REWIND

A HALF-CENTURY OF CLASSICS, CULT HITS, AND OTHER MUST-SEE MOVIES

COPYRIGHT © 2023 RICK ANDERSON
ALL RIGHTS RESERVED

No part of this book may be distributed, reproduced, or transmitted in any form or manner without the express written consent of the publisher, with the exception of brief passages to be used as quotes from a reviewer and certain other noncommercial uses as allowed by copyright law.

BOOK DESIGN
Alex Schloer

LIBRARY OF CONGRESS CONTROL NUMBER
2023911348

ISBN
978-0-578-38293-7

FIRST EDITION

graybearbooks.com
TACOMA, WASHINGTON

TO MY LATE BROTHER, JACK,
WHO INSPIRED MY LOVE FOR CLASSIC MOVIES
—FAMOUS AND OTHERWISE.

TABLE OF CONTENTS

INTRODUCTION i	KISS OF DEATH 79
3:10 TO YUMA 1	A LEAGUE OF THEIR OWN 82
ABSENCE OF MALICE 4	THE LEMON DROP KID 85
ANATOMY OF A MURDER 7	A LETTER TO THREE WIVES 88
APOLLO 13 10	MARRIED TO THE MOB 91
BAD DAY AT BLACK ROCK 13	MIRACLE ON 34TH STREET 94
THE BIG CHILL 16	MURPHY'S ROMANCE 97
THE BIG COUNTRY 19	THE MUSIC MAN 100
BRIGHT VICTORY 22	MY FAVORITE YEAR 103
BROADCAST NEWS 25	A PASSAGE TO INDIA 106
BYE BYE BIRDIE 28	PRESUMED INNOCENT 109
THE CAINE MUTINY 31	QUIZ SHOW 112
THE CANDIDATE 34	REAR WINDOW 115
CHINA MOON 37	RIO BRAVO 118
THE COURT JESTER 40	THE SET-UP 121
CROSSFIRE 43	SOUNDER 124
A DATE WITH JUDY 46	THE STING 127
DAVE 49	TALL STORY 130
THE DAY THE EARTH STOOD STILL 52	THEY WERE EXPENDABLE 133
THE DESPERATE HOURS 55	THE THIRD MAN 136
DRIVE A CROOKED ROAD 58	TWELVE O'CLOCK HIGH 139
EIGHT MEN OUT 61	THE VERDICT 142
GLORY 64	WRITTEN ON THE WIND 145
GOODFELLAS 67	ZERO HOUR! & AIRPLANE! 148
THE GREAT ESCAPE 70	INDEX 153
I CONFESS 73	PHOTO CREDITS 167
JOHNNY TREMAIN 76	ACKNOWLEDGEMENTS 169
	ABOUT THE AUTHOR 170

INTRODUCTION

Before I go into what this book is, an explanation is necessary as to what it is not: The films reviewed here do not represent anyone's listing of the top 50 in cinematic history. Just a pair of my selections, *Rear Window* and *GoodFellas*, made the American Film Institute's top 100.

Those two plus *Rio Bravo*, *The Third Man*, and *Written on the Wind* are the only five also to appear in legendary critic Roger Ebert's *The Great Movies* series of books, which covered roughly 400 films.

The Sting is the only one within my book to have won the Academy Award for Best Picture.

For that matter, just three of them (*Rear Window*, *Broadcast News*, and possibly *The Sting*) crack my personal top 10 list.

My exclusion of commentary on so many film classics is largely intentional. Truly great movies such as *Citizen Kane*, *Casablanca*, *Psycho*, *The Godfather*, and *Chinatown* have been dissected so thoroughly that it is difficult to believe I could bring anything fresh to the discussion.

I am not a conventional film critic. The bulk of my fifty-year journalism career has been spent as a sportswriter and editor for *The Daily World* newspaper in Aberdeen, Washington. But because I acquired a love for vintage movies from my late brother, Jack, who owned an extensive home video collection, my bosses generously permitted me to submit periodic movie reviews. Some of the pieces in this book previously have appeared (in altered form) in the newspaper.

Perhaps because my background is unorthodox, my sensibilities differ from those of traditional film critics and historians. I am not, for example, an unconditional admirer of such iconic directors as Martin Scorsese, Robert Altman, or Woody Allen (although they've all made some movies I like). While admittedly in a small minority, I also consider such renowned films as *Gone With the Wind, Vertigo, The Searchers, Moonstruck,* and *Fargo* overrated. Since film criticism is highly subjective, I would not argue with admirers of those movies—well, most of them.

Although the films in this collection were made during a fifty-year period (1945-95), that does not mean I consider this time period representative of a golden age of movies. It is simply the period with which I am most familiar.

In addition to reviewing their entertainment value, I have attempted to put many of these films in historical context—do we look at them and the performers differently now than we did at the time of release? That is the type of perspective Ebert provided so well in his *Great Movies* series.

You might notice some genres are underrepresented here. I am not much of a fan of science fiction, superhero action-adventures, or melodramas, nor of films in which the primary purpose is to push a political or social agenda. Not that there are no worthwhile films that fit these categories. I am just not the right person to review them.

The titles that made it into this collection represent a mixture of:

- outstanding productions that were shortchanged by Academy Awards voters (*Apollo 13, Broadcast News,* and *Presumed Innocent,* to name three);
- mostly forgotten quality films (*Eight Men Out, Bright Victory, Drive a Crooked Road*);
- guilty pleasures (*A Date With Judy, China Moon, The Lemon Drop Kid*); and
- ambitious misfires (*The Big Country, I Confess*).

In addition, I always have been fascinated by good films that could have been better (*The Caine Mutiny, The Desperate Hours,* and *Quiz Show*).

The common denominator is that I view them all as interesting movies that deserve to be watched at least once—and revisited.

Due primarily to my indecision about writing this book (which included at least one false start), it took me several years to complete it. This would not have been possible without several of my former co-workers at *The Daily World*.

Jeff Burlingame, whom I hired long ago as a sports clerk and who since has become a national award-winning author, helped inspire me to follow through on this project. Janet Simmelink, who edited the first drafts of many of these reviews, demonstrated that tough editing was not incompatible with a forty-year friendship. Kat Bryant did early edits for this book and provided invaluable assistance in getting it published.

Thanks as well to two former *Daily World* editors, Doug Barker and John Hughes: Doug for encouraging me to keep writing movie reviews following my retirement as sports editor, and John for being my friend and mentor throughout my journalism career. Now Washington state's chief historian, John made every writer he worked with better.

Finally, a confession: Readers might assume that fifty films encompassing a fifty-year period represents a carefully chosen theme. As every aspiring journalist is taught, one should never assume. My original draft included some seventy-odd films. It was only after I cut the list down that I realized the final fifty fit neatly within a fifty-year span. So that is a coincidence.

Hopefully, it will be an enjoyable one for readers. ■

3:10 TO YUMA

1957

DIRECTOR: DELMER DAVES

PRODUCER: DAVID HEILWEIL

SCREENPLAY: HALSTED WELLES FROM A SHORT STORY BY ELMORE LEONARD

STARRING: GLENN FORD AS BEN WADE, VAN HEFLIN AS DAN EVANS

RUNNING TIME: 92 MINUTES

The fascinating thing about the 1957 Western *3:10 to Yuma* is how little agreement it generates.

Rotten Tomatoes gives it a 96 percent approval rating. Legendary film critic Roger Ebert regarded it as both superior to the iconic *High Noon* and inferior to its own 2007 remake.

Although two stars of the time — legendary actor John Wayne and renowned director Howard Hawks — disliked *3:10 to Yuma* because the heroes beg for help from unreliable or unqualified bystanders, most observers rank the 1957 film as one of the era's most essential Westerns.

Based on an Elmore Leonard short story and directed by Delmer Daves, the film includes some gunplay and killings, but it is more of a psychological character study than an action picture.

Glenn Ford stars as Ben Wade, the leader of a highly organized gang of outlaws operating in Arizona. Ben intends to rob a stagecoach of a gold shipment without resorting to violence, but winds up fatally shooting the driver when he resists.

A dalliance with a barmaid (Felicia Farr) leads to Ben's arrest. Aware that the gang will stop at nothing to free its leader, the sheriff and stage owner devise an elaborate ruse that involves switching coaches and hiding Ben in a hotel room. There, he will be guarded by farmer Dan Evans (Van Heflin), who has been deputized for the mission. Dan is expected to keep Ben from escaping from the hotel room before escorting the outlaw to the titular train bound for a federal prison in Yuma.

Dan is a reluctant participant, to put it mildly. A hard-working if somewhat slow-witted family man left impoverished by a three-year drought, he joins the posse only for the $200 stipend offered by the stage owner.

While they wait in the hotel room for the train to arrive, the charming-but-ruthless Ben attempts to psych Dan out with a variety of ploys to secure his release. Meanwhile, Ben's gang—which operates with the efficiency of a Fortune 500 company—is headed to the rescue.

The interaction between Ben and Dan forms the foundation of the film.

Ben is the smarter of the two and knows what buttons to push. But, possibly to regain the respect of his family and his own self-esteem, Dan proves a tougher customer and more duty-bound than anticipated.

This film was remade exactly fifty years later by director James Mangold, with a cast headed by Russell Crowe as Ben and Christian Bale as Dan. It also received favorable notices.

While acknowledging the quality of the original, Ebert believed the remake better because, as he wrote on his website, *RogerEbert.com*, "[I]t has better actors with more thought behind their dialogue."

Bale is an exceptional actor, but so was fellow Oscar winner Heflin, who spent two decades mastering a wide range of big-screen roles. Most film historians

> ### "I DON'T GO AROUND SHOOTING PEOPLE DOWN. I WORK QUIET, LIKE YOU."
> — GLENN FORD AS BEN WADE

would rate Crowe above Ford, but the latter (who was switched from the role of the hero to the villain at his own request) gives perhaps his finest performance in creating a character who hides a cold-blooded and calculating nature behind an affable exterior.

The remake might boast a better supporting cast, with Ben Foster giving an Oscar-nominated turn as Ben's dedicated but half-crazed second-in-command. But the original film has its virtues as well, including a haunting title song sung by Frankie Laine over the opening credits. Leora Dana, a stage and TV actress who usually played unsympathetic parts on the big screen (she was Frank Sinatra's social-climbing sister-in-law in *Some Came Running*), delivers a quietly affecting performance as Dan's deglamorized wife—a woman who might be worn out by the family's hand-to-mouth existence, but nonetheless is loyal to her flawed husband.

The remake is twenty-five minutes longer than the original—not necessarily an asset in that the 1957 film's lean storytelling enhanced the tension—and contains several important plot changes. The difficulties in the Evanses' marriage are more explicitly delineated, and the attitude of their teenage son is altered from subtle disappointment in his father to outright contempt.

Then there is the new ending, accurately described by critic Leonard Maltin as a mixed blessing. If nothing else, it begs the question of whether the original's crowd-pleasing but wildly improbable conclusion is better than the remake's slightly more believable but less-satisfying climax.

Like many things about *3:10 to Yuma*, there is no consensus. ∎

ABSENCE OF MALICE

1981

DIRECTOR: SYDNEY POLLACK

PRODUCERS: SYDNEY POLLACK AND RONALD SCHWARY

SCREENPLAY: KURT LUEDTKE

STARRING: SALLY FIELD AS MEGAN CARTER, PAUL NEWMAN AS MICHAEL GALLAGHER

RUNNING TIME: 116 MINUTES

Some critics have suggested that *Absence of Malice* should be viewed as part of a double feature with *All the President's Men*—a pairing of movies depicting bad and good journalism.

As the "bad" half of that equation, *Absence of Malice* might also serve as a worthwhile companion piece to co-star Paul Newman's legal drama from the following year, *The Verdict*.

For all the furor that it generated among members of the media, the earlier film probably depicts newspaper reporting as accurately as *The Verdict* does the law.

The Verdict is superior, however, because it makes no pretensions to anything other than entertainment. In attempting to make a broader statement, *Absence of Malice* screenwriter Kurt Luedtke and director Sydney Pollack resort to the same type of half-truths and generalizations as the journalists they decry.

Sally Field co-stars in the drama as Megan Carter, a reporter for a fictional Miami newspaper. She has been assigned to follow up on the Jimmy Hoffa-like disappearance of a prominent Florida labor leader.

With the case at a standstill, the leader of a presumably federal strike force (one weakness of Luedtke's script is that he never makes clear the affiliations of the various investigators) leaks information to Megan via an unattended file on his desk. That information links Miami liquor distributor Michael Gallagher (played by Newman) to the crime.

The strike force chief does not necessarily believe that Michael, a presumably legitimate businessman, is guilty of abduction or murder. But he does think that, since Michael's late father was a bootlegger/loan shark and his uncle is a prominent mafioso, he might know more about the case than he is revealing.

By publishing the story with only a half-hearted attempt to contact Michael, the newspaper sets into motion a tragic chain of events in which Michael's alibi witness (Melinda Dillon) commits suicide.

That, in turn, prompts Michael to hatch a complicated plan (which includes romancing Megan) designed to exact revenge on those indirectly responsible for the woman's death.

A political liberal who likely had no problem with the *Washington Post*'s reporting on Watergate, Newman joined the production with surprising zeal—contending that the press often was irresponsible and that 90 percent of the stories written about him were inaccurate.

To his credit, onetime Detroit journalist Luedtke does not engage in that type of polemic. Nearly everything Megan writes in this film is accurate or presented to her as the truth.

The newspaper, embodied by an incredibly slipshod editor (Josef Sommer), is nevertheless culpable for failing to implement the checks and balances necessary for responsible journalism. Contrast the editor's recklessness in green-lighting partially sourced stories in this film with the Ben Bradlee character's careful editing in *All the President's Men*.

Megan, meanwhile, is guilty of prematurely publishing a defamatory story,

> **"EVERYBODY IN THIS ROOM IS PRETTY SMART, AND EVERYBODY IS DOING THEIR JOB. AND TERESA PERRONE IS DEAD ... WHO DO I SEE ABOUT THAT?"**
> — PAUL NEWMAN AS MICHAEL GALLAGHER

unnecessarily identifying the witness in exceptionally specific terms, making one-on-one contact with Michael following the suicide (and being assaulted for her trouble), revealing her original source, and then sleeping with another source.

Any reporter who made those kinds of mistakes would be fired. Megan, however, not only remains employed at the end of the film but is recommended for promotion by her clueless editor.

Newman and Dillon were nominated for Academy Awards, but it is the casting of Field that makes the film work. Her likable on-screen persona gives the reporter a human dimension that such harder-edged actresses such as Jane Fonda or Faye Dunaway might have failed to provide. It is doubtful, in fact, that Fonda or Meryl Streep would have agreed to play such a naïve character.

Absence of Malice contains a dynamic climactic scene in which a crusty Justice Department attorney (Wilford Brimley) assembles the principals and colorfully skewers all except Michael.

Unfortunately, the studio insisted upon a concluding scene that suggests a possible romantic reconciliation between Megan and Michael.

Let's see: Michael blames Megan for the death of his longtime friend. She, on the other hand, would be hooking up with a man who not only assaulted her but willfully destroyed her reputation.

Sounds like another mistake. ■

ANATOMY OF A MURDER

1959

DIRECTOR: OTTO PREMINGER

PRODUCER: OTTO PREMINGER

SCREENPLAY: WENDELL MAYES, BASED ON A NOVEL BY ROBERT TRAVER

STARRING: JAMES STEWART AS PAUL BIEGLER, LEE REMICK AS LAURA MANION

RUNNING TIME: 160 MINUTES

Briefly banned in Chicago for its frank discussion of sexual assault, *Anatomy of a Murder* was one of the most provocative movies of its era.

It would be no less controversial if remade today, but for an entirely different reason.

Not surprisingly, the courtroom drama was produced and directed by Otto Preminger, a filmmaker notorious for pushing the envelope on censorship. But it also starred

James Stewart, about the last actor you would expect to see in a movie that some deemed objectionable.

Stewart plays Paul Biegler, an attorney in a small town on Michigan's Upper Peninsula (where the film was shot). At loose ends after losing a re-election bid for county prosecutor, he spends most of his days fishing and his nights in boozy discussions of the law with an alcoholic older attorney (played by Arthur O'Connell).

Then a sensational murder case unexpectedly drops into his lap. He agrees to defend Frederick Manion (Ben Gazzara), a young Army lieutenant who shot and killed popular local innkeeper Barney Quill about an hour after Barney allegedly raped Manion's wife, Laura (Lee Remick).

To paraphrase the defense counsel in *The Caine Mutiny*, this is a case Paul probably wishes he were prosecuting.

There is no doubt Lt. Manion pulled the trigger in front of witnesses. The gap between the alleged rape and shooting gave him time to consider his actions. Arrogant and hot-tempered, with a history of domestic violence, the lieutenant is far from a sympathetic defendant.

And while Paul might be more than a match in the courtroom for his rather feckless successor as prosecutor, a brilliant and ruthless assistant state district attorney (George C. Scott) is recruited to assist in the prosecution.

Paul bases his defense on a form of temporary insanity known as "irresistible impulse," but his chief objective is to convince the jury that his client was morally, if not legally, justified in avenging his wife's honor.

While the subject matter was daring in 1959, modern audiences might wonder what all the fuss was about. The rape never is depicted (there are no flashback scenes) and is discussed more clinically than sensationally.

Many of today's viewers would be outraged, however, by the appallingly outdated suggestion that the rape victim enticed the attack.

Although Laura assures Paul that she has never given her husband cause for jealousy ("not once, not ever"), she dresses provocatively and makes no secret of her fondness for alcohol and the company of other men.

In his 1995 book *Oscar A to Z: A Complete Guide to More Than 2,400 Movies Nominated for Academy Awards,* Charles Mathews wrote that Preminger "... often brought energy and imagination to his films, evident here in the casting."

No kidding. The cast here is a mixture of veteran performers (Stewart, O'Connell, Eve Arden), and screen newcomers (Remick, Gazzara, Scott).

> **"I'M JUST A HUMBLE COUNTRY LAWYER TRYING TO DO THE BEST I CAN AGAINST THIS BRILLIANT PROSECUTOR FROM THE BIG CITY OF LANSING."**
> — JAMES STEWART AS PAUL BIEGLER

Preminger even found a role for Boston attorney Joseph N. Welch, best known for helping to take down Sen. Joseph McCarthy in the Army-McCarthy hearings. Although far from a trained actor, Welch is surprisingly effective as the trial judge.

While Stewart, O'Connell, and Scott received Academy Award nominations (this was the only such nomination Scott did not publicly reject), Remick was inexplicably omitted from the Oscar sweepstakes.

Cast only after Lana Turner dropped out of the film due to conflicts with Preminger, Remick found nuances in her character that the other actress probably would have missed. Remick is credible both as a woman confident in her sexuality and as a terrified, vulnerable victim.

Stewart, meanwhile, stretches his standard screen persona to portray a deceptively crafty attorney who is smarter than he is perceived, but happy to play the underdog in order to win the sympathies of the jury.

His casting also creates an interesting dynamic that Preminger is eager to exploit. Because likable Jimmy Stewart is playing the part, you root for his character to acquit a client who probably is guilty.

The chief knock against the movie is its one hundred and sixty-minute run time. (It is almost forty-five minutes before Paul even agrees to take the case.) But Preminger's pacing is so adroit and Wendell Mayes' screenplay so compelling, the film never seems bloated.

One of the first productions to take a realistic, even jaundiced, view of the law (an attitude that extends to a deliciously ironic concluding scene), *Anatomy of a Murder* proved a remarkably influential film. It inspired scores of like-minded movies and television shows, and was screened in some law-school classes.

Not bad for a movie once banned in Chicago. ■

APOLLO 13

1995

DIRECTOR: RON HOWARD

PRODUCER: BRIAN GRAZER

SCREENPLAY: WILLIAM BROYLES, BASED ON THE BOOK *LOST MOON* BY JIM LOVELL AND JEFFREY KLUGER

STARRING: TOM HANKS AS JIM LOVELL, KEVIN BACON AS JACK SWIGERT, BILL PAXTON AS FRED HAISE

RUNNING TIME: 139 MINUTES

I am far from an authority on space travel, yet I was impressed by the 1995 film *Apollo 13*.

More importantly, the film impressed me because it impressed my late brother, Jack.

A Boeing Co. aerospace engineer who was part of the ground crew for several unmanned space flights, Jack took strong exception to most cinematic portrayals of space exploration.

He dismissed the majority of such movies as unrealistic and was offended by the cynical tone that pervaded the critically acclaimed 1983 blockbuster *The Right Stuff*.

Jack acknowledged, however, that *Apollo 13* did the subject justice. That was a remarkable endorsement, since the re-creation of the ill-fated 1970 moon mission was dotted with potential landmines. Director and co-producer Ron Howard managed to avoid them even without resorting to NASA's archival footage and other offers of technical support.

The film begins with the selection of astronauts Jim Lovell (played by Tom Hanks), Fred Haise (Bill Paxton), and Ken Mattingly (Gary Sinise) to pilot the Apollo 13 craft to the moon. After being exposed to German measles, Mattingly is replaced by Jack Swigert (Kevin Bacon).

Although it had been only a year since Neil Armstrong became the first person to walk on the moon while commanding Apollo 11, the public's appetite for space flights had begun to wane. The Apollo 13 crew soon learned that the media response to the mission was underwhelming.

That all changed on the third day of the flight, after Lovell memorably tells the ground crew, "Houston, we have a problem."

One of the spacecraft's oxygen tanks explodes, setting off a chain reaction of malfunctions that force NASA officials to abort the scheduled moon landing. That is the least of their problems, since the lives of the astronauts also are in grave danger.

The astronauts, the Mission Control crew and even Mattingly (who assists with some simulations after his health is cleared) race against time to produce a safe return to Earth.

A real-life space buff, Hanks gives the story a solid foundation by replicating Lovell's calm leadership. The film, however, is far from a star vehicle. The supporting cast here is exceptional.

Kathleen Quinlan brings added grit to what could have been a stock part as Lovell's wife, Marilyn. Ed Harris might be even better as the chain-smoking, no-nonsense flight director, Gene Kranz. When he tells his co-workers, "Failure is not an option" and, "I believe this will be our finest hour," you believe him. Harris and Quinlan received Academy Award nominations in the supporting categories.

Astonishingly, though, Howard was excluded from the Best Director nominees. It is difficult to think of too many successful films in which the director played a greater role. Determining that every shot of the film would be original, Howard

> ## "HOUSTON, WE HAVE A PROBLEM."
> — TOM HANKS AS JIM LOVELL

presided over meticulous and realistic reconstruction of the spacecraft and the control-room sets, and he made great use of computer-generated special effects.

The onetime child star also mastered some small details that only informed viewers such as my brother would notice. He utilized footage, for example, of the controversial gloom-and-doom reports of ABC television's Jules Bergman to relate the darker moments of the rescue operation, but switched to Walter Cronkite's more optimistic coverage to accompany the triumphant conclusion.

Although the screenplay takes a few dramatic licenses (there were no verbal confrontations among the astronauts onboard, for example), Howard seemed to realize that fact, in this case, was more dramatic than fiction. He even created suspense in a climactic outcome that the vast majority of the audience already knew was coming.

Howard finally did receive an overdue Academy Award—for his direction of the 2001 historical drama *A Beautiful Mind*.

But even he—and my brother—might have agreed that *Apollo 13* represented his finest hour. ∎

BAD DAY AT BLACK ROCK

1955

DIRECTOR: JOHN STURGES

PRODUCER: DORE SCHARY

SCREENPLAY: MILLARD KAUFMAN, BASED ON THE SHORT STORY *BAD TIME AT HONDA* BY HOWARD BRESLIN

STARRING: SPENCER TRACY AS JOHN MACREEDY, ROBERT RYAN AS RENO SMITH

RUNNING TIME: 81 MINUTES

Some people regard *Bad Day at Black Rock* as a Western, though it is set in 1945 with nary a cowboy in sight. It is not exactly a film noir, either.

Perhaps it could be classified as a thriller with a social message—one that was not fully appreciated at the time of release.

Set in the immediate aftermath of World War II, the film opens with a train arriving in the Southwestern desert hamlet of Black Rock—the first time it has stopped there in four years. (Do not ask why the railroad has not eliminated the stop.)

Debarking is John Macreedy (played by Spencer Tracy), a war veteran who lost an arm in combat. He is seeking the whereabouts of Komoko, a Japanese American farmer who once lived outside Black Rock.

The panicked reactions of the townsfolk, harboring a guilty secret, make it clear that this is an appointment unlikely to be kept.

John is not only kept in the dark about Komoko's fate, but also is threatened by the menacing town leader, Reno Smith (Robert Ryan), and harassed by two of Reno's goons (Ernest Borgnine and Lee Marvin).

Quickly realizing that the weak, alcoholic sheriff (Dean Jagger) will not be of much help, John reacts passively to most of the intimidation. But he is no pushover, and it becomes evident that he will have to resort to some of his combat skills to get out of Black Rock alive.

Lean and mean at eighty-one minutes, *Bad Day at Black Rock* works as an exceptional suspense film and largely was considered as such upon its release. Today, it is probably best remembered as the first Hollywood movie to address the treatment of Japanese Americans during and after World War II.

The message horrified the aging MGM studio president, Nicholas Schenck, who labeled the plot subversive. But Dore Schary, the studio's liberal chief of production, was so enthusiastic about the story that he produced the film.

World War II attitudes about the enemy died hard in those days. It would be another two years before a reasonably sympathetic treatment of the German military, the submarine thriller *The Enemy Below,* made it to the big screen.

Bad Day at Black Rock benefited from late revisions. The gripping opening scene, in which an aerial shot tracks the speeding train thundering across the desert to the accompaniment of André Previn's pulsating musical score, replaced a less effective alternative that drew negative responses from preview audiences.

John Sturges, who received his only Academy Award nomination for this film, was not the first choice to direct. Even the title was different from its short story source, *Bad Time at Honda* (the change was made to avoid confusion with *Hondo,* the 1953 John Wayne Western).

I once suspected that the fifty-five-year-old Tracy—too old to be a combat veteran in a recently completed war and too short to be called a "big man" by another character—was not the original choice to star. There is no evidence, however, to

> **"FOUR YEARS AGO, SOMETHING TERRIBLE HAPPENED HERE. WE DID NOTHING ABOUT IT, NOTHING."**
> — WALTER BRENNAN AS DOC VELIE

support that view. On the contrary, the late film historian and Turner Classic Movies host Robert Osborne observed that Tracy had to be cajoled into playing the role, with studio executives floating false rumors that Alan Ladd (an actor even shorter than Tracy) was ready to be cast.

As it developed, Tracy was an inspired selection. A master of underplaying whose best performances came when he did not appear to be acting, he skillfully hides his character's steely resolve behind a passive exterior.

The celebrated fight scene in which he uses martial arts to subdue the burly Borgnine seems ludicrous on paper. But it is so well-staged that it appears realistic on the screen.

Considering that cast members Tracy, Borgnine, Marvin, Jagger, and Walter Brennan eventually won eight Academy Awards among them (although none for this film), it is not surprising that this is an exceptionally well-acted movie. Screenwriter Millard Kaufman also earned an Oscar nomination.

John's motivation for visiting Black Rock is not revealed until nearly the seventy-five-minute mark. Less than ten minutes later, he is back on the train (this time headed for Los Angeles), with the sympathetic town undertaker (played by Brennan) attempting to convince him that his stay might have changed Black Rock for the better.

With many in the town dead or under arrest, however, it is hard to believe a rebuilding effort is imminent.

The audience senses, in fact, that even a good day at Black Rock might not be all that great. ■

THE BIG CHILL

1983

DIRECTOR: LAWRENCE KASDAN

PRODUCER: MICHAEL SHAMBERG

SCREENPLAY: LAWRENCE KASDAN AND BARBARA BENEDEK

STARRING: GLENN CLOSE AS DR. SARAH COOPER, KEVIN KLINE AS HAROLD COOPER, WILLIAM HURT AS NICK CARLTON

RUNNING TIME: 103 MINUTES

For audiences of a certain age, *The Big Chill* is known for having perhaps the greatest title sequence ever. And it is even better for those who are aware of what is by now a relatively well-known piece of trivia.

The comedy-drama opens with several characters receiving distressing news and packing for a trip—all to the accompaniment of Marvin Gaye's rendition of "I Heard It Through the Grapevine."

Those scenes are intercut with tight shots (the character's face is never shown) of someone evidently dressing. Only at the end of the sequence is it revealed that the body is a corpse being dressed for a funeral that the other characters will attend.

The kicker for contemporary audiences is that the deceased, a suicide victim, was played by a then-unknown Kevin Costner. That is his body in the title sequence. But, aside from a blink-and-you'll-miss-it flashback scene near the conclusion, that is Costner's only appearance in the film. His other scenes were edited out of the finished product.

The character's suicide sets the story in motion. The dead man, Alex Marshall, was the charismatic leader of a group of student activists at the University of Michigan.

His friends traveling to the funeral in South Carolina include Nick (played by William Hurt), a cynical Vietnam veteran and former radio psychologist who now deals drugs; Michael (Jeff Goldblum), a smarmy magazine writer; Meg (Mary Kay Place), a disillusioned attorney; Sam (Tom Berenger), an actor who plays a swinging private detective on a television series; and Karen (JoBeth Williams), an unhappily married stay-at-home mother.

Hosting this group for a long post-funeral reunion weekend are Dr. Sarah Cooper (Glenn Close) and her businessman husband (Kevin Kline), whose marriage survived her brief affair with Alex. Also on hand is Chloe (Jennifer Tilly), Alex's childlike live-in girlfriend.

The group will spend the weekend sharing revelations and reflecting on the assorted directions their post-graduate lives have taken. At the end of the weekend, some of these lives will be altered, but most will maintain status quo.

The movie was directed and co-written by Lawrence Kasdan, a filmmaker whose work (*Body Heat, The Accidental Tourist,* and *Grand Canyon,* among others) tends to sharply divide critics. *The Big Chill* is no exception.

Detractors called it pointless, plotless, and overly reliant on attractive performers and classic period music such as "You Can't Always Get What You Want," "My Girl," and "Joy to the World" to cover its shortcomings. Strong similarities also were noted between this film and John Sayles' low-budget 1980 production, *Return of the Secaucus Seven.*

Yet *The Big Chill* is almost irresistible to those who attended college in the 1960s and early 1970s, mainly because its characters are so well-developed and recognizable. If there is a subtext of regret that they sacrificed their ideals for

> ### "I WAS AT MY BEST WHEN I WAS WITH YOU PEOPLE."
> — GLENN CLOSE AS DR. SARAH COOPER

materialism, there is also recognition that the choices they made were understandable and even inevitable.

In addition, the movie is just plain fun to watch. There is plenty of humor, and it never seems forced.

Close received an Academy Award nomination, and Hurt aces the film's flashiest part, but there is not a weak link in the cast. That might not have been the case had Costner's role been retained.

After reviewing the first cut, Kasdan said he eliminated most of Alex's flashback scenes because he thought the audience would have difficulty believing that so many people cared so deeply about this character.

That was viewed by some as an indictment of Costner's acting, but it really was not. The role required an actor who would be convincing as a magnetic rebel—someone like Johnny Depp or a young Jack Nicholson, for example. It simply did not fall into the understated Costner's wheelhouse.

In any event, Costner almost certainly came out ahead on the deal. As a type of makeup call, he was given an attention-getting supporting role in Kasdan's 1985 retro-Western, *Silverado*—a part that launched him to stardom.

Perhaps unknowingly, Kasdan employed a different type of anti-establishment figure when he cast Don Galloway in *The Big Chill* in the small role of Karen's straitlaced, disapproving husband. Best known as Raymond Burr's sidekick in the television police drama *Ironside*, Galloway gave up acting several years after this movie, moved to New Hampshire, and embraced the libertarian political philosophy.

In newspaper columns he wrote for the ultra-conservative *Manchester Union-Leader*, he called for New Hampshire's secession from the union and likened federal taxation to slavery.

Had Galloway been allowed to write his own lines, *The Big Chill* might have generated even more heat. It is doubtful, however, that a film depicting a reunion of college libertarians would have been half as entertaining. ■

THE BIG COUNTRY

1958

DIRECTOR: WILLIAM WYLER

PRODUCERS: WILLIAM WYLER AND GREGORY PECK

SCREENPLAY: JAMES R. WEBB, SY BARTLETT, AND ROBERT WILDER, BASED ON THE BOOK *AMBUSH AT BLANCO CANYON* BY DONALD HAMILTON

STARRING: GREGORY PECK AS JIM MCKAY, JEAN SIMMONS AS JULIE MARAGON, CHARLTON HESTON AS STEVE LEECH

RUNNING TIME: 166 MINUTES

The sprawling Western *The Big Country* might best be classified as a would-be epic.

Well-acted and very well-directed, the film has all the earmarks of a classic. But even though they never publicly acknowledged it, director William Wyler and star Gregory Peck (who also co-produced the film) seemed to be shooting for the ultimate pacifist Western. They fall a bit short, becoming victims of excessive length and their own lofty ambitions.

Peck plays Jim McKay, a ship's captain from Baltimore who travels west to marry Pat Terrill (Carroll Baker), the daughter of wealthy rancher

Maj. Henry Terrill (Charles Bickford). This is a couple who should have spent more time getting to know each other.

Upon his arrival, Jim finds himself in the middle of a longstanding feud between the major and his hardscrabble neighbor, Rufus Hannassey (Burl Ives). He also is harassed by Rufus' drunken offspring and challenged to various tests of manhood by Steve Leech (Charlton Heston), the major's surly, contemptuous foreman, who also has designs on Pat.

When Jim does not respond to most of those challenges, he loses the respect of his fiancée—to the point where it appears he might be a better match for Pat's schoolteacher friend, Julie Maragon (Jean Simmons), who owns land coveted by both the Terrills and the Hannasseys.

The stalwart Peck was an ideal choice to play a character who believes there are alternatives to violence. His attitude puts him in stark contrast to the macho landowners.

The major comes across as a more ruthless version of television's Ben Cartwright. Rufus is equally vengeful and a lot cruder, but he possesses a moral code of sorts that his rival lacks.

Ives won a Supporting Actor Academy Award for this film (although many observers believe he was honored in part for an equally acclaimed portrayal of Big Daddy in the film version of *Cat on a Hot Tin Roof* from the same year). Bickford's performance is equally strong.

There also is fine work from Baker, playing a feisty young woman with an unnatural attachment to her father, and Heston, who drops his customary heroic posture to convincingly play a far less sympathetic character.

Heston, in fact, emerged as the biggest winner in this production. Already an established star, he accepted a supporting role (and fourth billing) solely for the opportunity to work with Wyler. He was rewarded with the lead role in Wyler's next film, *Ben-Hur*, which earned Oscars for both actor and director.

Wyler, who had begun his long career directing low-budget Westerns but had made only one film in that genre during the previous thirty years, chose to emphasize the vastness of the landscape in *The Big Country*.

Frequently, he pulls back the camera for long shots. When Jim finally accepts the foreman's invitation for a fistfight, Wyler shoots most of the confrontation from a nearby butte.

There also are some welcome flashes of humor (giving courtship advice to his

> **"NOW TELL ME, LEECH. WHAT DID WE PROVE?"**
> — GREGORY PECK AS JIM MCKAY, FOLLOWING A LONG FIGHT
> WITH CHARLTON HESTON AS STEVE LEECH

eldest son, Rufus casually suggests that he take a bath occasionally), and Jerome Moross contributes a memorably thunderous musical score that deserved (but did not win) an Oscar.

In short, there is a lot of good stuff here, but Wyler does not know when to quit. Although the three-time Oscar-winning director was noted for his pacing in such lengthy films as *Ben-Hur* and *The Best Years of Our Lives,* the story here is not as substantial.

The movie drags on for nearly three hours, eventually winding down to a climax that most discerning viewers could have predicted from about the one-hour mark.

When Peck's and Simmons' characters exchange meaningful glances in the final scene, they might have been thinking, "What was that all about?"

Friends since they collaborated on the romantic comedy *Roman Holiday* five years earlier, Wyler and Peck initially were enthusiastic about co-producing the movie. From the outset of shooting, however, they got along about as well as the Terrills and the Hannasseys—clashing over costs, cuts, and retakes.

According to Peck's biographer, Lynn Haney, Wyler's first cut of the film ran nearly four hours—a version that would have sent audiences scurrying for the exits. By that time, the director and the star no longer were on speaking terms. Wyler was quoted as saying he would not direct Peck again for a million dollars.

The two buried the hatchet a few years later, but never again worked together.

Once they resumed a civil relationship, they might have agreed that *The Big Country* was simply too big. ∎

BRIGHT VICTORY

1951

DIRECTOR: MARK ROBSON

PRODUCER: ROBERT BUCKNER

SCREENPLAY: ROBERT BUCKNER, FROM THE NOVEL *LIGHTS OUT* BY BAYNARD KENDRICK

STARRING: ARTHUR KENNEDY AS LARRY NEVINS, PEGGY DOW AS JUDY GREENE

RUNNING TIME: 97 MINUTES

Although it was a thoughtful, inspirational story about the rehabilitation of a disabled war veteran, *Bright Victory* is not a title that is familiar to all of today's movie buffs. If anything, many might confuse it with the 1939 Bette Davis tearjerker *Dark Victory*.

The film's anonymity reflects that of three of its stars. They include a Black actor whose career was impeded by a shortage of opportunities, an actress who willingly withdrew from the spotlight, and a talented actor who had everything but charisma.

The latter was Arthur Kennedy, a five-time Academy Award nominee who received a rare crack at a leading role in this film. He plays Larry Nevins, an Army sergeant who is blinded in combat during World War II.

With the aid of the staff at the Valley Forge General Hospital in Pennsylvania (where some scenes were shot), Larry learns to cope with his blindness. Repairing his personal life proves equally challenging.

He demonstrates some inbred racism during an early scene. Later, his casual use of the N-word costs him a friendship with Joe Morgan (played by James Edwards), a fellow patient whom he does not realize is Black.

Initially consumed by bitterness and self-pity, Larry also brushes aside Judy Greene (Peggy Dow), a bank employee who volunteers at functions for hospital patients.

Soon, however, Larry and Judy become friends and eventually fall in love. That poses another complication. Larry is engaged to Chris Paterson (Julia Adams), a wealthy young woman with whom he will reunite when he goes home to Florida for the first time since the accident.

As the plot summary suggests, Larry is not an entirely likable character. He is, however, capable of change. His self-discovery represents the film's foundation.

Based on a novel by Baynard Kendrick and directed by Mark Robson, *Bright Victory* is constructed in two parts.

The first, focusing on the procedures the hospital staff follows to prepare blind patients for their return to society, is filmed in semi-documentary form. The more personal touches come in the second half, as Larry attempts to adjust to life without sight.

To some extent, this film was the victim of bad timing. It was released only a year after producer Stanley Kramer staked out the same territory in *The Men*, which featured Marlon Brando in his big-screen debut as a paraplegic war veteran.

The Men has the better reputation today, but I like *Bright Victory* more, because its characters seem less stereotypical.

Adams, for example, plays a woman who is neither unrelentingly loyal nor brutally thoughtless. She is supportive and loving, but also fearful of the adjustments she will be forced to make in her lifestyle if she marries Larry.

The cast is universally fine. One of the first Black actors to play multidimensional characters, Edwards made *Bright Victory* only two years after what

> **"I TOLD YOU I WANTED SECURITY. WELL, I WAS LOOKING FOR IT IN ALL THE WRONG PLACES."**
> — ARTHUR KENNEDY AS LARRY NEVINS

should have been a star-making role in the World War II drama *Home of the Brave*. His part is much smaller here, but he plays it with his customary sensitivity.

Hampered by his liberal politics during the blacklisting era and the general lack of meaningful roles for Black actors, his career already was beginning to wane. Three years later, he was reduced to playing an uncredited role as a ship's steward scooping sand into a tureen during the famed strawberries scene in *The Caine Mutiny*.

Dow's brush with stardom was even more short-lived. Immensely appealing in this film as a woman whose compassion gradually turns to love, she might have forged a substantial career in wholesome roles. But, after three more films, she left Hollywood to marry an Oklahoma oilman. The marriage lasted sixty years, during which she became a noted philanthropist.

Any actor playing a character with disabilities attracts attention, but Kennedy truly is superb. An actor of exceptional range who played everything from idealists to rapists, he effortlessly masters the complexities of this character.

He beat out the likes of Brando (for *A Streetcar Named Desire*) and Humphrey Bogart (for *The African Queen*) to win the New York Film Critics Best Actor award, although he lost the Oscar to Bogart.

Yet Kennedy lacked the personal magnetism that attracted audiences and filmmakers. Although he proved here that he could carry a movie, he soon was back in supporting roles.

Actually, *Bright Victory*'s supporting cast is better known today than its stars. They include television veterans Will Geer (who plays Larry's father) and Jim Backus, plus a young Rock Hudson in a tiny role as a soldier.

The same director who cast Arthur Kennedy in a leading role presumably kills off Hudson's character (his fate is never referenced later) in the first five minutes—which might make Mark Robson both a good judge of acting talent and a bad judge of star power. ∎

BROADCAST NEWS

1987

DIRECTOR: JAMES L. BROOKS

PRODUCER: JAMES L. BROOKS

SCREENPLAY: JAMES L. BROOKS

STARRING: WILLIAM HURT AS TOM GRUNICK, HOLLY HUNTER AS JANE CRAIG, ALBERT BROOKS AS AARON ALTMAN

RUNNING TIME: 131 MINUTES

The scene most people remember from *Broadcast News* is the one in which Albert Brooks' character develops flop sweat while anchoring a weekend news broadcast. My personal favorite comes a few minutes later. Frustrated that his affection for Holly Hunter's character will remain unrequited, Brooks ticks off a long list of reasons she should not fall for the handsome anchorman played by William Hurt.

He concludes it with "... and I'm in love with you!" He then pauses before adding: "How do you like that? I buried the lead."

Viewers who believe that no actual person would say such a thing have never spent much time around journalists.

Fortunately, writer-director James L. Brooks knows better. His film about the inner workings of network television news is both funny and insightful. But it works best as a character study folded inside a love triangle.

Hunter plays Jane Craig, a smart, talented producer whose compulsion for organization even includes scheduling brief daily crying sessions.

Albert Brooks is her ostensibly platonic friend Aaron Altman, a gifted reporter whose network career has been hindered by his lack of charisma.

Hurt's character, Tom Grunick, a newcomer to the network, possesses the looks and magnetism that Aaron lacks. Although he is no intellectual giant and admits that he does not always understand the news he is reporting, he is clearly on the fast track to success—and the inside track to Jane's affections.

The strength and, curiously, the weakness of James Brooks' screenplay is that these people emerge as three-dimensional characters.

Aaron, for example, is intelligent and dedicated (he even phones in suggestions for a breaking story he has been excluded from covering), but also is abrasive and condescending to Tom.

The latter, likable and aware of his shortcomings, initially comes across as more sympathetic. But he also is ambitious and not above using his looks and charm to further his career—even if it means bending journalistic standards.

Meanwhile, the same perfectionism that makes Jane a crackerjack producer has left her personal life in shambles. When a co-worker played by Joan Cusack tells her late in the film, "Except for socially, you're my role model," it is funny partly because it has the ring of truth.

Having gone to such lengths to demonstrate that neither Aaron (a man she does not romantically love) nor Tom (whom she does not respect) is right for Jane, James Brooks paints himself into a corner in resolving the situation.

He settles for an epilogue that lamely intends to tie up the personal and professional loose ends.

The three leads all received deserved Oscar nominations. It is hard to imagine anyone other than Albert Brooks playing the neurotic, sardonic Aaron. Hurt would not have been everyone's first choice to portray a beefcake newsman, but

> **"...HE PERSONIFIES EVERYTHING YOU'VE BEEN FIGHTING AGAINST. AND I'M IN WITH LOVE WITH YOU. HOW DO YOU LIKE THAT? I BURIED THE LEAD."**
> — ALBERT BROOKS AS AARON ALTMAN, TO HOLLY HUNTER AS JANE CRAIG

he gives what could have been a stock character unusual substance. The character of Jane Craig was written for Debra Winger (the co-star of James Brooks' Oscar-winning *Terms of Endearment*), but she dropped out after becoming pregnant. The change in casting was probably for the better.

While the talented Winger easily could have captured Jane's intensity, it is doubtful she could have replicated the vulnerability and poignancy that Hunter brought to the role.

With seven unsuccessful nominations, *Broadcast News* was a notorious Academy Awards washout. The now mostly forgotten epic *The Last Emperor* harvested the bulk of the major trophies, while Norman Jewison's ethnic comedy *Moonstruck* received most of the others.

I probably am in the minority in my belief that *Broadcast News* was far superior to both those films. I will acknowledge, however, that there were some understandable reasons for the Oscar-night snubs.

James Brooks' screenplay, a much gentler commentary on the foibles of TV news than 1976's *Network*, might have been considered too derivative of the television hit *The Mary Tyler Moore Show*, which Brooks helped create.

The writer-director had won three Oscars for *Terms of Endearment* only four years earlier. Also, *Broadcast News* was released earlier in the year than the other leading contenders.

Only in the Best Actress category was the voting inexplicable. If 100 acting coaches were assembled to judge the performances, I'd be surprised if ten favored Cher, the winner for *Moonstruck*.

Cher might have been honored for exceeding expectations in a charming but far less demanding role than Hunter's. Although Hunter received a Best Actress statuette for *The Piano* six years later, her loss here remains one of the Academy's all-time worst calls.

Awards or not, *Broadcast News* is a great movie.

How do you like that? I buried the lead. ■

BYE BYE BIRDIE

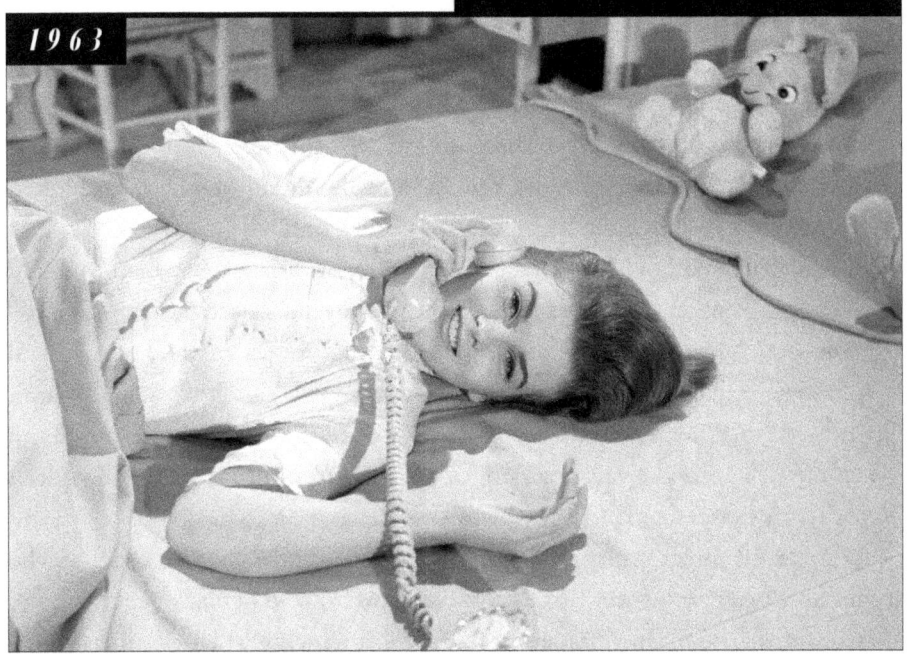

1963

DIRECTOR: GEORGE SIDNEY

PRODUCER: FRED KOHLMAR

SCREENPLAY: IRVING BECHER, BASED ON THE BROADWAY MUSICAL BY MICHAEL STEWART, CHARLES STROUSE, AND LEE ADAMS

STARRING: DICK VAN DYKE AS ALBERT PETERSON, JANET LEIGH AS ROSIE DELEON, ANN-MARGRET AS KIM MACAFEE

RUNNING TIME: 112 MINUTES

The movie version of *Bye Bye Birdie* differs significantly from the earlier stage production. That is not necessarily better or worse, just different.

If nothing else, the 1963 screen musical demonstrates how the dynamics of a production can be transformed by a director's vision—or personal preferences.

Featuring music by Charles Strouse and Lee Adams and directed by Broadway legend Gower Champion, the 1960 stage play featured a handful of hit songs (including "Put On a Happy Face" and "I've Got a Lot of

Living to Do") while satirizing the furor that accompanied Elvis Presley's 1958 induction into the U.S. Army.

The Elvis proxy is rock singer Conrad Birdie, whose draft notice creates a crisis for songwriter/manager Albert Peterson and Albert's secretary/girlfriend, Rosie. The latter two hatch a scheme in which Conrad appears on *The Ed Sullivan Show* (then television's top-rated variety program) to perform Albert's latest song, "One Last Kiss." There he will bestow a farewell smooch on Kim MacAfee, an adoring teenage girl who is president of Conrad's fan club in a small Ohio town.

The financial windfall from the song's recording would enable Albert to escape his possessive mother and marry Rosie. But first they must contend with Conrad's ego, the show-business ambitions of Kim's father, and the jealousy of her boyfriend.

On stage, Albert was played by then-unknown Dick Van Dyke, with dynamic Broadway dancer Chita Rivera portraying Rose. Thanks to the success of his hit TV comedy, Van Dyke was retained for the film version, as was Paul Lynde as young Kim's exasperated father.

But veteran director George Sidney replaced Rivera with Janet Leigh—who might have been perfect for Rosie's role if you overlooked her lack of singing and dancing talent, not to mention her inability to convincingly play a Latina.

More fatefully, he cast Ann-Margret as Kim.

Undeniably impressed by and possibly infatuated with the young actress (in his autobiography, Van Dyke recalls her sitting on the director's lap between takes), Sidney set out to beef up what had been a distinctly supporting role on stage.

Ann-Margret was given songs that previously had been performed by other characters. Sidney used his own money (he subsequently was reimbursed by the studio) to film new opening and closing scenes in which she sings a title tune not included in the original production.

Other plot alterations were made. For the film, Albert is stripped of his managerial duties (a wise choice, in that the manager of a singer as popular as Conrad would not exactly be starving) and strictly is a struggling songwriter. His fallback profession also is changed from English teacher to biochemist, and he sings "Put on a Happy Face" not to a group of kids, as on stage, but to Rosie.

Kim's boyfriend is transformed from a nerd (originally played by Michael J. Pollard of *Bonnie and Clyde* fame) to a better-looking, more musically inclined suitor (played by pop singer Bobby Rydell).

The character of Kim originally was written as a star-struck small-town girl who

> ## "SPREAD SUNSHINE ALL OVER THE PLACE. JUST PUT ON A HAPPY FACE."
> — SUNG BY DICK VAN DYKE AS ALBERT PETERSON

learns the differences between fantasy and reality. While Ann-Margret makes a valiant attempt to capture the same degree of innocence, you can see the strain. The smoldering sexuality she displays in a couple of scenes is far more convincing.

Not all the changes work. As Van Dyke later wrote, "It was not the movie (Janet) signed on for and, as far as I was concerned, it was not the play."

Yet it is hard to say Sidney was wrong in shifting the film's focus. Ann-Margret injects the type of energy that neither the likable but bland Van Dyke nor the miscast Leigh can provide.

Meanwhile, the play's satire was already becoming dated by the time the film was made and seems far more so today. For all his self-destructive tendencies, Presley was, by most accounts, a nicer person than the hedonistic Conrad (played in the film by Jesse Pearson).

The original Broadway Birdie, incidentally, was played by Dick Gautier, who later earned a degree of cult fame as Hymie the Robot on television's *Get Smart*.

Wrapping up a 30-year film career highlighted by such good if not necessarily great musicals as *Annie Get Your Gun* and *Kiss Me Kate,* Sidney directed only one more popular movie after *Bye Bye Birdie*.

Appropriately, that is when he paired Ann-Margret with the real-life Elvis in 1964's *Viva Las Vegas*. ∎

THE CAINE MUTINY

1954

DIRECTOR: **EDWARD DMYTRYK**

PRODUCER: **STANLEY KRAMER**

SCREENPLAY: **STANLEY ROBERTS AND MICHAEL BLANKFORT, FROM THE NOVEL BY HERMAN WOUK**

STARRING: **HUMPHREY BOGART AS LT. CMDR. PHILIP QUEEG, JOSÉ FERRER AS LT. BARNEY GREENWALD, VAN JOHNSON AS LT. STEVE MARYK**

RUNNING TIME: **125 MINUTES**

When entertaining-but-flawed movies are discussed, my mind immediately turns to *The Caine Mutiny*.

The 1954 drama received seven Academy Award nominations, including one for Best Picture, and it remains compelling for audiences today. But it might have been a masterpiece had it not been for a couple of questionable decisions by the filmmakers.

The film actually was the final element in what might be described as a creative arts trilogy.

First came Herman Wouk's 1951 Pulitzer Prize-winning novel. That, in turn, spawned a hit Broadway play, *The Caine Mutiny Court-Martial*.

The challenge in adapting the story to film is that the book and play took dramatically different approaches.

Wouk's sprawling novel focused on Willis Keith, a wealthy, sheltered young man who becomes a naval officer during World War II. His service on the fictional Caine, a battered minesweeper stationed in the Pacific, has him growing from a callow ensign to the Caine's final captain.

But Keith is only a witness to the story's most dramatic episode. Lt. Steve Maryk, the ship's executive officer, relieves the mentally unhinged Capt. Philip Queeg of command when the Caine is in jeopardy of foundering during a typhoon. Maryk is eventually court-martialed for that action.

The play focuses solely on the trial—with Queeg, Maryk, and defense attorney Barney Greenwald (played on stage by Henry Fonda) as the primary characters.

For the film version, producer Stanley Kramer and director Edward Dmytryk opted for a compromise: The movie ends with the court-martial and its aftermath, but much of the plot revolves around Keith.

That might have worked with the right actor in the role; a young Anthony Perkins would have been a perfect choice. Instead, screen newcomers Robert Francis and Donna Hickey (who took the name of her character, May Wynn, for this and a handful of subsequent films) were cast as Keith and his nightclub singer girlfriend.

Since Francis was tragically killed in a plane crash the year after *The Caine Mutiny* was released, it would be nice to report that this film represented a lasting legacy to his acting talent. Alas, his performance is so wooden here, he makes Pinocchio seem like Robin Williams.

Wynn's character is supposed to be fiery, but instead comes across as whiny as she attempts to rid her boyfriend of his attachment to his mother. Their scenes together are almost cringe-inducing, particularly in comparison to the work of a powerhouse cast in the other key roles.

Humphrey Bogart plays Queeg, the unpopular captain who famously demonstrates his mental instability by rolling steel balls in his hands. Always at his best in portraying morally complex characters, Bogart makes Queeg seem more pathetic than villainous. Bogart received his final Oscar nomination in the process.

Bogart gets solid support from Van Johnson, as the earnest if none-too-bright

> "AH, BUT THE STRAWBERRIES. THAT'S WHERE I HAD THEM. THEY LAUGHED AT ME AND MADE JOKES. BUT I PROVED BEYOND A SHADOW OF A DOUBT AND WITH GEOMETRIC LOGIC THAT A DUPLICATE KEY TO THE WARDROOM ICEBOX DID EXIST."
> — HUMPHREY BOGART AS PHILIP QUEEG

Maryk, and José Ferrer, as the shrewd defense attorney who acknowledges he'd rather be prosecuting.

Fred MacMurray, playing nicely against type, gives one of his best performances as the cynical but spineless officer who undermines Maryk's confidence in the captain. He was unaccountably omitted from the Supporting Actor Oscar nominations.

These characters are so well-drawn and the shipboard and courtroom scenes so strong that the audience comes to resent the time devoted to Keith and his romantic interludes.

The problem was compounded by Columbia studio chief Harry Cohn's edict that none of his films would exceed two hours. *The Caine Mutiny* bends that rule, but only by five minutes. The story justified at least another thirty.

Although such subsequent Navy-themed movies as *A Few Good Men* and *Crimson Tide* contain some common elements, *The Caine Mutiny* has never been remade for the big screen.

That might be due in part to Wouk's curiously ambivalent point of view. After depicting Queeg as a tyrannical lunatic, the novelist eventually concludes that Maryk's actions were premature at best and could have been avoided with a little more mutual understanding.

Known for such socially conscious "message" pictures as *The Defiant Ones*, *Judgment at Nuremberg*, and *Guess Who's Coming to Dinner*, producer Kramer could not have been entirely comfortable with the theme of this film—particularly since the message in this case appears to be that it is OK for Navy crew members to sacrifice their lives in a typhoon as long as the chain of command is maintained.

But the real message of *The Caine Mutiny* is that when you have an entertaining story and an all-star cast, it is foolish to let untested actors carry the narrative. ∎

THE CANDIDATE

1972

DIRECTOR: MICHAEL RITCHIE

PRODUCER: WALTER COBLENZ

SCREENPLAY: JEREMY LARNER

STARRING: ROBERT REDFORD AS BILL MCKAY, PETER BOYLE AS MARVIN LUCAS

RUNNING TIME: 109 MINUTES

In a sense, it is a shame *The Candidate* is remembered primarily for its final line. Because it also might be the truest political movie ever made and contains one of Robert Redford's finest performances.

Redford stars as Bill McKay, a legal-aid attorney whom the Democratic Party recruits to challenge three-time California Republican Sen. Crocker Jarmon. The son of a former governor, an old-line machine politician, Bill is so jaded by the political process that he is not even registered to vote.

But political consultant Marvin Lucas (Peter Boyle) believes Bill's name familiarity and spotless liberal credentials might make him electable. In addition, as Bill's father notes at one point in the proceedings, "He's not going to get his ass kicked. He's cute."

Bill's first press conference, in which he speaks his mind on the issues, is a disaster. His early campaign appearances are not much better. When he tries to make political capital out of a wildfire by blaming it on neglect for the environment, he is quickly upstaged by Crocker's pledge to introduce a bill guaranteeing disaster insurance.

Although he gives Bill a note early in the campaign predicting that he'll lose, Marvin was not hired to preside over a defeat. He persuades the candidate to moderate his views to attract a broader political base—and sacrifice his ideals in the process.

Redford, who helped develop the movie with director Michael Ritchie, made two particularly smart decisions in the production. He hired Jeremy Larner, a former speechwriter for Sen. Eugene McCarthy, to author the screenplay and assigned himself to play the lead.

Although Redford's original vision was to depict Bill as a sellout, he was willing to compromise with Larner's less explicit statement in what turned out to be an Academy Award-winning screenplay.

What separates *The Candidate* from such heavier-handed political films as *All the King's Men* and *Primary Colors* is its subtlety. Bill does not undergo a dramatic transformation, but the audience can see him losing his principles inch by inch.

Larner also knows the campaign trail down to its last yard. From the drudgery of the campaign to the well-rehearsed speeches and awkward photo ops, the episodic screenplay ranks high in authenticity.

Many contemporary viewers assume that Bill's character was based on California Gov. Jerry Brown, the son of former Gov. Pat Brown. But the younger Brown did not take office for the first time until three years after this film was made. Bill more likely was a composite character, with former New York Mayor John Lindsay and California Sen. John Tunney (the son of heavyweight boxing champion Gene Tunney) supposedly the prime inspirations.

> ## "WHAT DO WE DO NOW?"
> — ROBERT REDFORD AS BILL MCKAY

A liberal political activist in his own right, Redford was a natural for the role. He finds the right notes to suggest Bill's compromises.

James Stewart was reportedly approached to play the incumbent senator, but disliked the film's unfavorable depiction of conservatives. That proved to be a blessing in disguise. Stewart's heroic public image—formed in part by playing the ultimate political idealist in *Mr. Smith Goes to Washington*—would have colored the character.

Veteran television actor Don Porter, the eventual choice, was ideal. He was smooth and savvy enough to be credible as a three-term senator, but reactionary enough to repel a significant portion of his constituency.

Boyle and Melvyn Douglas are very good as well. The latter, a veteran of real-life political battles through his marriage to Helen Gahagan Douglas (a former U.S. congresswoman who lost a bruising senatorial race to Richard Nixon), steals every scene he is in as the wolfish old-style pol who has an uneasy relationship with his son.

His triumphant declaration to Bill, "Son, you're a politician," might under ordinary circumstances have been the film's most memorable line. It is overshadowed, however, by the climactic question Bill poses to Marvin: "What do we do now?"

Redford, Ritchie, and Larner probably were wise to leave well enough alone in dealing with the candidate's political future.

But I cannot help thinking the same creative trio could have collaborated on a sequel, *The Senator,* that might have become a classic in its own right. ■

CHINA MOON

1994

DIRECTOR: JOHN BAILEY

PRODUCER: BARRIE M. OSBORNE

SCREENPLAY: ROY CARLSON

STARRING: ED HARRIS AS KYLE BODINE, MADELEINE STOWE AS RACHEL MUNRO

RUNNING TIME: 99 MINUTES

As is the case with a lot of things, timing is everything with movies.

Blessed with a taut story line, two excellent lead performances, and a late twist that I did not see coming, *China Moon* is one of my favorite modern films noir.

Yet its reputation has always suffered by comparisons to the more critically acclaimed *Body Heat*, released thirteen years earlier.

The audience response to *China Moon* on the Rotten Tomatoes website produced only a thirty-seven percent favorable rating. In his 2015 *Movie Guide*, Leonard Maltin dismissed it as "more than a little reminiscent of (the superior) *Body Heat*" and awarded it only two stars.

Maybe it is just me, but I'm not sure *Body Heat* is that superior. Still, both films are set in Florida, and the plots are admittedly similar.

Ed Harris has the starring role in *China Moon* as Kyle Bodine, a small-town police detective whose deductive powers and attention to detail make him a whiz at homicide investigations.

As he tells his rookie partner Lamar Dickey (played by a young Benicio Del Toro), criminals always make at least one stupid mistake. Kyle contemptuously compares the suspect in one investigation to a contestant on *The Gong Show*.

Kyle's workplace proficiency is not reflected in his bank account (he lives in a trailer home). Nor has it helped his social skills (he shows up for one date wearing mismatched socks).

But his lonely life takes an upturn when he encounters the glamorous Rachel Munro (Madeleine Stowe) in a lounge.

Unhappily married to the wealthy but abusive banker Rupert Munro (Charles Dance), she is amused by Kyle's clumsy pick-up lines before gently rejecting him. "You almost swept me off my feet," she tells him. That rejection, however, is so gentle that Kyle later seeks her out, and they eventually begin a relationship.

That makes things awkward when Kyle and Lamar are summoned to the Munro mansion to investigate a domestic violence incident. Several days later, Rachel fatally shoots Rupert under circumstances that could be interpreted as either self-defense or premeditated murder.

Fearful that the latter interpretation will prevail, a frantic Rachel persuades Kyle to help her cover up the shooting. He reluctantly agrees, even as evidence emerges implicating him in the crime.

The characterizations in this movie differ subtly but significantly from those in *Body Heat*.

Kyle is smarter and less complicit in the shooting than William Hurt's Ned Racine in the earlier film. Rachel is much more of a victim and less overtly manipulative than Kathleen Turner's Matty Walker. And while Matty's ill-fated husband (played by Richard Crenna) was not a particularly likable guy, he was a veritable saint compared to the arrogant, adulterous, abusive Rupert.

> **"IF YOU EVER LOVED ME, TRUST ME NOW."**
> — MADELEINE STOWE AS RACHEL MUNRO, TO ED HARRIS AS KYLE BODINE

An actor who can do little wrong in my book, Harris predictably masters the complexities of his character.

So does Stowe, an often-underrated actress. How Rachel really feels about Kyle is the key to the story's development. Her reaction to the climactic events partially salvages a needlessly violent final scene.

The ending is probably this film's weakest link. The plot twist, on the other hand, holds up on repeated viewings. Still, it is not clear what might have happened had Kyle accepted Rachel's initial rejection.

On second thought, perhaps a Plan B was unnecessary. As *Body Heat* also demonstrated, it is a given that lust always trumps logic in films noir. ∎

THE COURT JESTER

1955

DIRECTORS: NORMAN PANAMA AND MELVIN FRANK

PRODUCERS: NORMAN PANAMA AND MELVIN FRANK

SCREENPLAY: NORMAN PANAMA AND MELVIN FRANK

STARRING: DANNY KAYE AS HUBERT HAWKINS, GLYNIS JOHNS AS MAID JEAN

RUNNING TIME: 101 MINUTES

Although enormously popular in the 1940s and 1950s, Danny Kaye does not have the greatest reputation among 21st-century film buffs.

In a series of movie comedies he made during his heyday, Kaye tended to play the same character—a bashful schmo transformed (through impersonation or supernatural means) into a man of action.

A talented singer and an acclaimed performance artist, he could be funny in the right vehicle. His manic comedy style, however, sometimes resembled Robin Williams on a bad day.

Kaye is probably best remembered for playing Bing Crosby's army buddy in the 1954 holiday classic *White Christmas,* and the title character in the 1952 musical biography *Hans Christian Andersen.*

Most film historians agree, however, that Kaye's cinematic masterpiece was *The Court Jester*—one of the funniest films of the era and a rare big-screen spoof that is every bit as entertaining as its inspiration. In it, Kaye stars as Hubert Hawkins, an ex-carnival performer who joins a band of good-hearted rebels in medieval England.

The king has taken power through illicit means but failed to kill an infant who is the rightful heir to the throne. The rebels have the child in their custody, but are forced to transport him to safety when his whereabouts become known.

Denied a combat role by the group's leader, the Black Fox, Hubert is assigned to join Maid Jean (played by Glynis Johns) in taking the infant to a secure location. He winds up gaining access to the royal court by impersonating the newly hired jester.

Once at the castle, Hubert becomes involved in no fewer than three subplots.

Maid Jean, with whom he has fallen in love, says she will marry him if he can help the Black Fox overthrow the king. Sir Ravenhurst (Basil Rathbone), the king's treacherous right-hand man, wants the jester to assassinate his rivals. And Princess Gwendolyn (Angela Lansbury) sees Hubert as a possible alternative to an arranged marriage to the boorish Sir Griswold (Robert Middleton).

Then there is Griselda (Mildred Natwick), Gwendolyn's witchlike consort, who casts a spell that will turn the meek jester into a swashbuckler with a snap of her fingers.

It does not take a film expert to determine that this plot is a send-up of the 1938 classic *The Adventures of Robin Hood.* But screenwriters Norman Panama and Melvin Frank, who also produced and directed, do not slavishly follow the earlier film's story. The Black Fox, for example, bears scant resemblance to Errol Flynn and is very much a minor character.

Panama and Frank instead build the plot around Kaye's standard comic routines and patter songs (the latter composed by Kaye's wife, Sylvia Fine Kaye). It works this time—largely because much of the material is legitimately funny and in part because the story is more substantial than the typical Kaye fare.

The film is best remembered for the tongue-twisting "the pellet with the

> **"THE PELLET WITH THE POISON'S IN THE VESSEL WITH THE PESTLE. THE CHALICE FROM THE PALACE IS IN THE BREW THAT IS TRUE."**
> — MILDRED NATWICK AS GRISELDA THE WITCH, REPRISED BY DANNY KAYE AS HUBERT HAWKINS

poison's in the vessel with the pestle" scene, in which Griselda attempts to tell Hubert which one of two drinks is poisoned. Although Kaye was identified with this scene for the rest of his life, it actually is Natwick who flawlessly delivers the bulk of the dialogue.

The supporting cast is unusually strong for a Kaye film. Johns, Lansbury, Natwick, and Cecil Parker (who plays the king) were skilled comedic performers.

The real casting coup, however, was landing the sixty-four-year-old Rathbone to essentially re-create the same villainous role he played in *The Adventures of Robin Hood*.

An accomplished fencer, Rathbone received additional pay for instructing Kaye, a novice with the sword. He might have done his job too well. A natural athlete, Kaye quickly became so proficient that it was Rathbone who was forced to use a stunt double for the climactic duel.

Writer-directors Panama and Frank also were known for their association with Bob Hope. For much of the movie, it is easy to imagine Hope playing Hubert. But he almost certainly couldn't have matched Kaye's athleticism in the action scenes.

Despite its critical acclaim, *The Court Jester* tanked at the box office. Kaye's film career spiraled rapidly downward thereafter (although his 1961 World War II comedy, *On the Double,* was a largely unseen gem). He did restore his reputation as the star of an Emmy Award-winning television variety series in the 1960s, *The Danny Kaye Show*.

A passionate baseball fan, Kaye became part of the original ownership group of the Seattle Mariners in 1976. Five dismal seasons later, he sold his interest in the team—probably wondering all the while why he had not hired Griselda the witch to cast a spell that would have transformed the Mariners into the New York Yankees. ■

CROSSFIRE

1947

DIRECTOR: EDWARD DMYTRYK

PRODUCER: ADRIAN SCOTT

SCREENPLAY: JOHN PAXTON, FROM THE NOVEL *THE BRICK FOXHOLE* BY RICHARD BROOKS

STARRING: ROBERT MITCHUM AS SGT. PETER KEELEY, ROBERT YOUNG AS CAPT. FINLAY, ROBERT RYAN AS MONTY MONTGOMERY

RUNNING TIME: 86 MINUTES

On a list of 1940s films that were subsequently remade, *Crossfire* is curiously absent. Curious, in that the subject seems more topical than ever.

While the 1947 drama contained a powerful anti-discrimination message, a return to the original source might make it even more powerful for today's audiences.

The story was based on future screenwriter-director Richard Brooks' 1945 novel, *The Brick Foxhole*, which focused on homophobia in the military. Hollywood's Production Code at the time, however, forbade any reference to homosexuality, so screenwriter John Paxton changed the identity of a murder victim from gay to Jewish.

The film was a critical and financial success, earning five Academy Award nominations. But now, with gay themes no longer taboo and hate crimes still very much in the news, it is easy to imagine the same scenes working even better with a more faithful adaptation of Brooks' story.

No apologies were necessary, however, for the movie that was made.

The story opens with the beating death, shown in silhouette, of salesman Joseph Samuels (played in flashback scenes by Sam Levene) in a Washington, D.C., hotel room.

Police initially suspect an emotionally troubled army corporal, who was seen with Samuels in the hotel bar and later in his room. But viewers (particularly those who are good at identifying silhouettes) quickly become aware that a more likely culprit is Monty Montgomery (Robert Ryan), a bellicose ex-soldier with a history of hostility toward minorities. The trick is nailing Monty before he can cover his tracks—or kill again.

Although cast against type, Robert Young underplays nicely as the weary, pipe-smoking homicide detective who resorts to a clever ruse to trap the killer.

Robert Mitchum, who raised underplaying to an art form, breezes through his undemanding role as an army sergeant who aids in the investigation in hopes of clearing the corporal.

There are also juicy supporting roles for Oscar-nominated Gloria Grahame as a tough young woman the corporal meets in a bar, and Paul Kelly as the mysterious older man who might be her husband (or her pimp).

But the standout performance belongs to Ryan, who had some history with the material.

Not yet established as a major Hollywood actor, Ryan had read the novel while serving in the Marines and lobbied Brooks for the role before the movie rights were even optioned.

Getting his wish was a mixed blessing. His performance helped launch a long film career while earning him his sole Oscar nomination. But it also typecast the actor, a dedicated liberal and noted humanitarian off-screen, as a specialist in playing sociopaths.

Ryan's ability to create such an authentic character is what makes the role so memorable. Most viewers have encountered someone like Monty—a guy who can

> **"IGNORANT MEN ALWAYS LAUGH AT THINGS THAT ARE DIFFERENT—THINGS THEY DON'T UNDERSTAND. THEY'RE AFRAID OF THINGS THEY DON'T UNDERSTAND. THEY END UP HATING THEM."**
> — ROBERT YOUNG AS CAPT. FINLAY

clear a bar with his loud opinions. It is an open question, however, whether this bully intended to merely beat up Samuels or actually kill him.

If there is a weakness in the story, it is Monty's later conversion to a more calculating murderer. Given his fear of exposure in the early scenes, I'd peg him as more of a flight risk than a serial killer.

The film's status as a groundbreaking production might have been greater had it not been made simultaneously with another movie about anti-Semitism, *Gentleman's Agreement*.

Pushed by RKO studio chief Dore Schary, *Crossfire* producer Adrian Scott and director Edward Dmytryk completed their film first. But the makers of *Gentleman's Agreement* got the last laugh when that movie won the Best Picture Academy Award.

Some firm historians argue that *Crossfire*'s Oscar chances were torpedoed when Scott and Dmytryk were blacklisted for alleged Communist ties. Perhaps so, but *Gentleman's Agreement* was the more prestigious production and a more explicit attack on anti-Semitism—factors that usually resonate with Academy voters.

Crossfire, however, has aged more gracefully. *Gentleman's Agreement* is filled with long, self-important speeches and even contains a subplot on writer's block—an element that is about as entertaining as it sounds.

Tightly packaged at eighty-six minutes, *Crossfire* delivers its message more directly and suspensefully and benefits from Dmytryk's film-noirish staging of key scenes almost entirely in shadow.

In short, *Crossfire* was a quality film for its time. More than 70 years later, it might be time to try it again with a different approach. ■

A DATE WITH JUDY

1948

DIRECTOR: RICHARD THORPE

PRODUCER: JOE PASTERNAK

SCREENPLAY: DOROTHY COOPER AND DOROTHY KINGSLEY FROM THE RADIO SERIES BY ALEEN LESLIE

STARRING: JANE POWELL AS JUDY FOSTER, ELIZABETH TAYLOR AS CAROL PRINGLE

RUNNING TIME: 113 MINUTES

Admittedly a guilty pleasure, *A Date With Judy* is a featherweight musical comedy with a plot that can charitably be described as farfetched.

It is redeemed, however, by its high spirits and eclectic cast.

How eclectic? Try Elizabeth Taylor, Robert Stack, singing ingenue Jane Powell, 1930s tough guy Wallace Beery, Brazilian bombshell Carmen Miranda, and bandleader Xavier Cugat.

It is almost impossible to envision all these people in the same production. Astonishingly, though, the film succeeds almost in spite of itself.

The movie actually is based on a popular 1940s radio show, but it was tailored to fit the talents of its stars.

Powell plays the title character, Judy Foster, a high school student and musical prodigy with a lovestruck boyfriend named Oogie Pringle (Scotty Beckett). Their relationship is compromised when Oogie's older sister, Carol (played by Taylor), advises him to feign indifference by sending a surrogate to take Judy to the prom.

Insulted and crestfallen, Judy drowns her sorrows at a local soda fountain (a sure sign this film is set in the 1940s). There she falls hard for Stack's character, Steve Andrews, a college student moonlighting as a soda jerk. Steve is prodded into escorting Judy to the prom, but then meets and becomes smitten with the beautiful Carol.

Meanwhile, Judy's father (Beery) is secretly taking dance lessons from a nightclub entertainer (Miranda) in order to surprise his wife for their anniversary. In ninety-nine percent of screen comedies, such clandestine meetings are misinterpreted by others. It is not exactly a spoiler alert to suggest this is no exception.

Even if you accept the notion of Elizabeth Taylor dispensing relationship advice, the story here easily could have spawned a bad sitcom. But Richard Thorpe directs it affectionately and breaks up the plot with a surprisingly healthy helping of memorable musical numbers.

Although Miranda was past her prime as a box-office attraction, her rendition of "Cuanto la Gusta" became her biggest hit. Powell delivers one of her signature songs, "It is a Most Unusual Day," and teams with Beckett for a cute novelty number, "Strictly on the Corny Side."

The diverse cast generates a nice rapport. While Powell indicated in her autobiography that the aging, cantankerous Beery was disliked by most of the cast and crew, it does not show on screen. The scene in which Miranda teaches him to rumba is one of the film's highlights.

Taylor and Powell, who became friends off-screen, are convincing as teens who can remain civil despite competing for the same man.

Powell also enjoys good chemistry with the long-forgotten Beckett, a onetime child star whose adult career was curtailed—and his life tragically shortened—by drug and alcohol problems. (The somewhat similar 1949 musical *Nancy Goes to*

> ## "IT'S A MOST UNUSUAL DAY. IT'S LIKE CATCHING THE BRIDAL BOUQUET."
> — SUNG BY JANE POWELL AS JUDY FOSTER

Rio, in which producer Joe Pasternak reunited the couple, was less successful in part because Beckett played a much smaller role.)

Pushing thirty, Stack was a little mature to be playing a college student—albeit one who presumably had his education interrupted by military service. Fortunately, Thorpe underplays his romance with Taylor, who was playing an eighteen-year-old character but was barely sixteen when the film was released.

Needless to say, all the romantic subplots are neatly resolved by the time Judy closes the film by reprising "It's a Most Unusual Day."

When she impulsively tells Oogie at the climax that she forgives him for everything, the audience has almost forgotten why she was mad at him in the first place.

A Date With Judy might be a cheap date. Sometimes, though, those can be fun, too. ■

DAVE

1993

DIRECTOR: IVAN REITMAN

PRODUCERS: IVAN REITMAN AND LAUREN SHULER DONNER

SCREENPLAY: GARY ROSS

STARRING: KEVIN KLINE AS DAVE KOVIC AND PRESIDENT BILL MITCHELL, SIGOURNEY WEAVER AS ELLEN MITCHELL

RUNNING TIME: 110 MINUTES

Perhaps because it is difficult to satirize one part of the political process without alienating a portion of the audience, few successful political satires have come out of Hollywood.

Both a critical and box-office success, *Dave* could be regarded as one of the best of the genre, except for the minor detail that it really is not a satire.

Instead, screenwriter Gary Ross and director Ivan Reitman chose to soft-pedal the politics and turn the film into an enjoyable romantic comedy, set against a political backdrop.

Kevin Kline stars as Dave Kovic, the amiable owner of a temporary job placement service in Washington, D.C. He supplements his modest income doing impressions of his lookalike, President Bill Mitchell (also played by Kline).

That avocation attracts the attention of the president's aides, who ask Dave to impersonate the president leaving a political function. He's told the ruse is for vague security purposes, but it is really to allow the president to sneak off for an assignation with one of his secretaries (a young Laura Linney).

Complications develop when the president is left comatose by a stroke suffered during lovemaking. Bob Alexander (Frank Langella), the president's manipulative chief of staff, views the tragedy as an opportunity to seize power.

Keeping the president's incapacity secret, Bob convinces Dave to continue doubling for the president for an indefinite period. That would give Bob sufficient time to frame the vice president (Ben Kingsley), a genuinely honorable man, on trumped-up charges, then have himself appointed vice president—and eventually ascend to the Oval Office when the president's condition becomes public knowledge.

Dave is understandably skeptical that he can pull this off, particularly in being able to fool First Lady Ellen Mitchell (Sigourney Weaver). No problem, he is told. The president and first lady no longer share the same bedroom and are barely on speaking terms, thanks to his numerous affairs and his indifference to the social programs she has championed.

Unaware of Bob's Machiavellian motives, Dave agrees to the subterfuge. Far more personable than the president, he wins over the press and public while improving the conservative president's image.

Ellen quickly identifies Dave as an imposter, but discovers she likes the ersatz president better than the real one. But Dave makes an enemy of Bob when he decides to make some policy changes.

This premise, most memorably filmed 56 years earlier in the Ronald Colman classic *The Prisoner of Zenda,* requires a huge suspension of disbelief from the audience.

Even with that, several major plot holes exist: While they might look alike, it would seem highly improbable that Dave and the president would have similar voices. Wouldn't Linney's character, virtually forgotten for the second half of the film, want to continue her relationship with the president? Could an imposter such as Dave really fire an actual chief of staff?

> **"I FORGOT THAT I WAS HIRED TO DO A JOB FOR YOU, AND IT WAS JUST A TEMP JOB AT THAT."**
> — KEVIN KLINE AS DAVE KOVIC

Ross and Reitman have some fun with a liberal-in-conservative's-clothing early on, recruiting some real-life politicians, journalists, and entertainers for cameo roles (Wyoming Sen. Alan Simpson has a particularly funny sound bite).

There also is a memorable sequence in which Dave recruits an accountant friend (Charles Grodin, in a bit part) to help trim the budget so the government can maintain operation of a homeless shelter for children.

But the filmmakers do not appear comfortable pushing a political agenda. Consequently, the second hour focuses more on the growing attraction between Dave and Ellen and their attempts to outwit Bob.

It helps that there are accomplished performers in the key roles. The regal, self-assured Weaver, an actress who radiates intelligence even when she is pursuing aliens, makes an ideal first lady. The glowering Langella is a suitably treacherous villain.

A celebrated stage actor who performed in everything from Shakespeare to musicals on Broadway, Kline did not make his film debut until his mid-30s, when he was hand-picked by Meryl Streep to play her ill-fated lover in *Sophie's Choice*.

His habit of rejecting many big-screen parts earned him the nickname "Kevin Decline." Perhaps that selectivity, however, helped him bring a fresh approach to the roles he accepted. His exuberance in this film makes the audience believe he could fool the media—and woo a disillusioned first lady.

If there were any doubt that *Dave* is more fantasy than satire, it is dispelled in a final scene that might be the most farfetched in the movie. But it also is the ending the majority of the audience wants.

As any politician can attest, bipartisan popularity beats credibility every time. ∎

THE DAY THE EARTH STOOD STILL

1951

DIRECTOR: ROBERT WISE

PRODUCER: JULIAN BLAUSTEIN

SCREENPLAY: EDMUND NORTH

STARRING: PATRICIA NEAL AS HELEN BENSON, MICHAEL RENNIE AS KLAATU

RUNNING TIME: 92 MINUTES

With few exceptions, I'm not much of a science-fiction movie fan. The original version of *The Day the Earth Stood Still* is one of those exceptions.

Credit an unusually mature approach to the material and a perfectly cast lead actor.

Spencer Tracy and Claude Rains were among those reportedly considered for the role of Klaatu, the alien from an unknown planet who arrives in Washington, D.C., via a flying saucer to deliver a pacifist ultimatum.

Either actor probably would have done a decent job (although it is difficult to imagine Tracy, the quintessential American everyman, playing someone from another planet). But their distinctive screen personalities might have been a distraction.

Fortunately, producer Julian Blaustein and 20th Century Fox studio chief Darryl F. Zanuck settled on British actor Michael Rennie.

Already in his 40s when this film was made, the tall, gaunt Rennie was far from a newcomer to the big screen. He had started appearing in British films in the mid-1930s and even had a couple of American-made productions under his belt.

He was, however, a relative unknown to U.S. audiences—an asset for the role of an invader from outer space. In addition, his reserved but authoritative acting style was ideal for his character.

The science fiction genre was just beginning to take hold in American cinema. But even the more ambitious early entries in that class were usually poorly acted scare-fests dominated by special effects.

This film was one of the first of its type to treat the audience as adults.

Zanuck assigned first-class talent to the project. Director Robert Wise (a believer, incidentally, in UFOs), screenwriter Edmund North, composer Bernard Herrmann, and actress Patricia Neal all won Academy Awards at some point during their respective careers.

The film opens with the arrival of the spaceship on the National Mall. Accompanied by the robot Gort (played by 7-foot-7 Lock Martin), Klaatu exits the spacecraft to proclaim that he has come in peace.

He nevertheless delivers a stern message for earthlings: Attack other nations if you must, but refrain from unleashing atomic weapons against other entities in the solar system.

The consequences for ignoring this warning could be severe. The giant robot is capable of zapping entire armies with a single ray from his eye visor. At one point, the otherwise dignified Klaatu wonders aloud whether he should level New York City or sink the Rock of Gibraltar to demonstrate the seriousness of his intent.

With the U.S. Army and various governments taking a dim view of his proposal, Klaatu assumes the identity of "Mr. Carpenter" (one of the film's several Christlike allusions) and takes up residence in a Washington boarding house.

> ## "KLAATU BARADA NIKTO."
> — PATRICIA NEAL AS HELEN BENSON

There he strikes up a friendship with young war widow Helen Benson (Neal) and her son (Billy Gray).

Eventually, the frustrated Klaatu elects to sidestep the government and take his case directly to a group of international scientists gathering in Washington for a summit. The army, however, has other ideas.

Rennie's casting provides for the unfulfilled suggestion of a romantic relationship between Klaatu and Helen—an element that would have been lacking if Rains, for example, had played the lead.

Klaatu is attractive enough in human form to arouse the jealousy of Helen's boyfriend, Tom Stevens (played by Hugh Marlowe), an insurance salesman who sees exposing the alien as his ticket to fame and fortune.

When Helen pleads with him to remain silent, arguing that the fate of the world hangs in the balance, Tom utters the classic response, "I don't care about the rest of the world. You'll feel differently when you see my picture in the newspaper."

While Neal went on to forge a significant Hollywood career, Klaatu was not a star-making role for Rennie, though Fox executives initially thought it might be. They cast him as Jean Valjean the following year in one of the many screen adaptations of *Les Miserables*. When the reception to that film fell short of expectations, Rennie returned to supporting parts. By the 1960s, he was working primarily in television, including a stint as the villainous Sandman in the camp series *Batman*, prior to his death in 1971.

For all its other assets, *The Day the Earth Stood Still* might be best remembered for the line "Klaatu barada nikto," a message delivered by Helen to Gort.

The phrase's meaning has been extensively debated in the years since. Screenwriter North told film historian Steven Jay Rubin that it meant, "There is hope for the Earth, if the scientists can be reached."

In the context of the plot, however, that explanation makes little sense. The line is delivered after Klaatu has been gunned down by the army, but it contains no information about his condition or whereabouts.

For those without English-alien dictionaries, it remains one of cinema's greatest mysteries. ∎

THE DESPERATE HOURS

1955

DIRECTOR: WILLIAM WYLER

PRODUCER: WILLIAM WYLER

SCREENPLAY: JOSEPH HAYES AND JAY DRATLER FROM THE NOVEL BY HAYES

STARRING: HUMPHREY BOGART AS GLENN GRIFFIN, FREDRIC MARCH AS DANIEL HILLIARD

RUNNING TIME: 112 MINUTES

In panning the 1990 Anthony Hopkins-Mickey Rourke crime thriller *Desperate Hours,* many reviewers urged readers to instead watch the 1955 original, *The Desperate Hours,* which co-starred Humphrey Bogart and Fredric March.

Ironically, while viewing that very movie, I found myself wanting to check out an even earlier version of the same story.

Considering that it inspired a novel, a Broadway play, and two movies, it is not surprising that the story is a good one.

In the 1955 film, convict Glenn Griffin (played by Bogart) engineers an escape from an Indiana prison. Accompanied by his young brother, Hal, and the brutish convict Simon Kobish (Robert Middleton), Glenn takes temporary refuge in an Indianapolis home while awaiting the delivery of money from a female accomplice.

The home in question is occupied by businessman Daniel Hilliard (March), his wife (Martha Scott), and their two children—a nineteen-year-old daughter and an elementary school-aged son.

The criminals plan to stay only a few hours until the money arrives. But the courier is detected by police, forcing the gang to extend its stay and terrorize the family while devising a potentially lethal Plan B.

That in turn sets up a battle of wits between the wily but vicious Glenn and the haggard, calculating Daniel.

Director William Wyler has a top-notch supporting cast—Scott, Middleton, Arthur Kennedy, and Gig Young (as the boyfriend of Hilliard's daughter)—at his disposal. Middleton is particularly memorable as a brawny con who enjoys playing with children's toys and has plenty of toys in his own attic.

Most critics, however, reserved their greatest praise for the acting of old pros Bogart and March. That description is doubly apt.

Among the finest actors of their generation, Bogart and March were assuredly pros, and their performances here were up to their customary standard. And both were getting old—perhaps too old for their roles.

In his penultimate film, the fifty-five-year-old Bogart was twenty-three years older than Dewey Martin, the actor playing his brother. March was older still, at fifty-eight. For that matter, at forty-two, Young was old enough to be his screen girlfriend's father.

The casting becomes problematic given that the Broadway play staged the previous year co-starred Paul Newman (in Bogart's role) and Karl Malden (in March's).

In his late twenties and yet to make his film debut, Newman presumably was not a contender to re-create his stage part. Even after becoming established on the big screen, he was seldom asked to play outright villains. But his customary mixture of intelligence and intensity would have made him a good fit for Glenn.

Seventeen years younger than March, Malden would have brought a vitality to Daniel's character that his patrician, somewhat-theatrical film counterpart lacked.

A key moment in the climax comes when Glenn, confronted by a gun-wielding Deniel, tells the businessman, "You don't have it in you." March responds: "I've

> ## "I'VE GOT IT IN ME ALL RIGHT. YOU PUT IT THERE."
> — FREDRIC MARCH AS DANIEL HILLIARD, TO HUMPHREY BOGART AS GLENN GRIFFIN

got it in me all right. You put it there." That was believable enough, but Malden, specialist in conveying rage, probably would have been even more convincing.

Miscast or not, this is a worthwhile film. Wyler, who became a three-time Oscar winner, keeps the tension percolating throughout and seldom betrays the story's stage origins.

The play and movie were adapted from a 1953 novel. The book, in turn, was inspired by an actual incident in which a Philadelphia-area family was held hostage by a group of convicts for nineteen hours.

The real-life family sued *Life* magazine over an article on the play, contending that the magazine misrepresented the actual home invasion. Far from being threatened and assaulted, as the article suggested, family members said they were treated courteously by the cons.

When the case wound up going to the U.S. Supreme Court several years later, the family was represented by Richard Nixon, then in private law practice. (You cannot make up stuff like this.) The decision went in the magazine's favor—not Nixon's last loss before the high court.

Probably even Nixon would not have advocated for the movie to be remade with more fidelity to the facts. A film titled *The Courteous Hours,* in which the criminals and family exchanged pleasantries for nineteen hours, would not have drawn much of an audience. ∎

DRIVE A CROOKED ROAD

1954

DIRECTOR: RICHARD QUINE

PRODUCER: JONIE TAPS

SCREENPLAY: RICHARD QUINE AND BLAKE EDWARDS

STARRING: MICKEY ROONEY AS EDDIE SHANNON, DIANNE FOSTER AS BARBARA MATHEWS

RUNNING TIME: 82 MINUTES

One magazine in 1954 advertised *Drive a Crooked Road* as the best movie of the year. That would have ranked this now mostly forgotten film noir superior to the Academy Award-winning *On the Waterfront*—not to mention *Rear Window, The Caine Mutiny, Seven Brides for Seven Brothers,* and the Judy Garland version of a *A Star Is Born.*

While that is definitely a minority viewpoint, this is nonetheless an interesting, unusual noir. It features a screenplay by a filmmaker far better known for comedy, a femme fatale with a conscience, and an uncharacteristically subdued performance by its star.

That star is Mickey Rooney, only thirty-four years old at the time of filming but already at a career crossroads after a string of box-office disappointments. Here, he plays Eddie Shannon, a California auto mechanic who moonlights as a race-car driver and dreams of competing on the European circuit.

Lonely in his personal life and taunted at work about his short stature and lack of success with women, he is surprised to draw the attention of the seductive Barbara Mathews (played by Dianne Foster). She hires him to fix her car, then invites him to spend time with her away from the auto shop.

Barbara's true purpose, however, is to recruit Eddie to drive the getaway car for a bank robbery being plotted by her lover, Steve Norris (Kevin McCarthy), whom she introduces to Eddie as merely a platonic friend.

Eddie is smitten with Barbara and is further tempted by Steve's offer to finance his European racing ambitions. Barbara, however, begins to have second thoughts about her role in the scheme—not because she has fallen in love with Eddie, but because she feels sorry for him.

The screenplay was written by Blake Edwards, who was three years away from making his big-screen directorial debut and nine years from writing and directing his comedic mega-hit *The Pink Panther*.

Perhaps because he was relatively new to the trade, Edwards put a different spin on the material than most noir writers.

The majority of classic noirs, while entertaining, are not particularly realistic. But *Drive a Crooked Road* is populated with recognizable characters who make believable choices.

Normally bristling with energy even after he outgrew musicals with Judy Garland, Rooney is convincingly restrained in portraying a decent guy attempting to escape an unsatisfying life.

McCarthy is fine as the charming but amoral villain, as is Jack Kelly (later television's dashing Bart Maverick) in a rare unsympathetic role as Steve's cynical partner in crime.

The chief victim of the film's plunge into relative obscurity was Foster, a versatile Canadian-born actress who was making her American big-screen debut.

She's very good in a complicated role. But despite later working with such big-name stars as Spencer Tracy, James Stewart, and Burt Lancaster and such directors

> ## "HE'S NOT LIKE OTHER PEOPLE. HE'S LIKE A LONESOME LITTLE ANIMAL. HE'S NEVER HAD ANY LOVE IN HIS WHOLE LIFE."
> — DIANNE FOSTER AS BARBARA MATHEWS

as John Ford, she never found a niche in Hollywood and was relegated to television guest appearances by the early 1960s.

This film might have earned a better reputation with a more suitable director than Richard Quine, who also did the final adaptation of Edwards' screenplay. A former actor and boyhood friend of Rooney who enjoyed most of his success directing romantic comedies, Quine was not particularly adept at staging action scenes.

By short-circuiting the personal encounters between Eddie and Barbara (who never have anything approaching a love scene), Quine and Edwards also leave the audience with a key unanswered question: Is Eddie entirely delusional about their relationship, or does she give him some reason to believe they have a future together?

Even if it stalls in the pits occasionally, *Drive a Crooked Road* is a buried treasure worth uncovering at least once—particularly if you do not expect it to be a better film than *On the Waterfront*. ■

EIGHT MEN OUT

1988

DIRECTOR: JOHN SAYLES

PRODUCER: SARAH PILLSBURY

SCREENPLAY: JOHN SAYLES, BASED ON THE BOOK BY ELIOT ASINOF

STARRING: JOHN CUSACK AS BUCK WEAVER, D.B. SWEENEY AS JOE JACKSON, DAVID STRATHAIRN AS EDDIE CICOTTE

RUNNING TIME: 119 MINUTES

It has a downbeat story and a shortage of big-name stars, and it is based on events now more than 100 years old.

Why, then, does the historical baseball drama *Eight Men Out* still boast a cult following among some moviegoers?

Probably because of writer/director/actor John Sayles' storytelling skills and commitment to accuracy, plus the fine work of a splendid ensemble cast.

Sayles tells the story of the 1919 "Black Sox" scandal. Eight members of the American League champion

Chicago White Sox agreed to accept money from gamblers to intentionally lose the World Series to the Cincinnati Reds. All eight later received lifetime bans from baseball.

Although first baseman Chick Gandil was the acknowledged ringleader of the plot, Sayles focuses on three other conspirators.

Star pitcher Eddie Cicotte (played by David Strathairn) joins the fix after being denied a raise by skinflint owner Charles Comiskey (Clifton James). Illiterate slugger Shoeless Joe Jackson (D.B. Sweeney) goes along with the deal without recognizing its ramifications. Ultra-competitive third baseman Buck Weaver (John Cusack) won't rat on his teammates after learning of the plot, but plays to win nonetheless.

Dozens of other characters (ballplayers, sportswriters, and gamblers) also are introduced—an attention to detail that represents both the film's strength and its weakness.

The size of the cast is true to the enormity of the operation. But because Sayles was under a studio mandate to keep the film under two hours (he made it with one minute to spare), he was forced to introduce the characters at a breakneck pace.

Viewers without a solid grounding in baseball history would be well-advised to replay the opening twenty minutes. Otherwise, it is tough to tell the players without a scorecard.

Like most of Sayles' films, this one has a socially conscious message. The writer-director makes a compelling case that the poorly educated players, in contrast to today's multimillionaire athletes, were victims. In his telling of the story, they were exploited by a ruthless owner and out of their league in dealing with the wily gamblers—particularly the cold-blooded gangster Arnold Rothstein (Michael Lerner).

Cusack gives a suitably intense performance as Weaver, who is trapped between team loyalty and a desire to win. Strathairn, a regular in Sayles films, is even better as the conscience-stricken Cicotte.

Sayles, who often acted in his own productions, convincingly plays legendary writer Ring Lardner. Chicago-based author Studs Terkel is surprisingly effective as another sportswriter covering the story. Other familiar names in the cast include Charlie Sheen, John Mahoney, and Christopher Lloyd.

In a year-end survey of critics conducted by *USA Today*, *Eight Men Out* received the highest rating of any 1988 film. It was a failure at the box office, however, and was shut out of Academy Award nominations.

> **"YOU SAY YOU CAN FIND (EIGHT) MEN ON THE BEST TEAM THAT EVER TOOK THE FIELD WILLING TO THROW THE WORLD SERIES? I FIND THAT HARD TO BELIEVE."**
> — KEVIN TIGHE AS GAMBLER SPORT SULLIVAN

The film was a labor of love for Sayles, who spent several years struggling to obtain financing for the project. Closely following the details outlined in Eliot Asinof's painstakingly researched book, also titled *Eight Men Out,* his fidelity to the reported facts is almost total.

The period details and action sequences are also authentic—although, curiously, the players often react to key hits and errors more like Little Leaguers than seasoned pros.

Since the film was released, however, some baseball historians have taken issue with Asinof's account of the scandal.

In his only published interview on the topic, Gandil acknowledged his complicity but contended that the White Sox were beaten in some games they intended to win. Despite the film's depiction of the White Sox as a juggernaut, a few historians have suggested that the Reds actually fielded the superior team.

Weaver's role in the fix also has been disputed, with one source asserting that he came up with the very bad idea of taking the money and then double-crossing the gamblers.

One of the film's few fictional scenes is one of its best. Banned from baseball, Weaver watches Jackson play in a semi-pro game under an assumed name but refuses to acknowledge his ex-teammate's identity.

That incident never happened. But it provides a suitably sad coda to a movie that, like the 1919 Cincinnati Reds, never received its due. ■

GLORY

1989

DIRECTOR: EDWARD ZWICK

PRODUCER: FREDDIE FIELDS

SCREENPLAY: KEVIN JARRE, BASED ON THE BOOKS *LAY THIS LAUREL* BY LINCOLN KIRSTEIN AND *ONE GALLANT RUSH* BY PETER BURCHARD

STARRING: MATTHEW BRODERICK AS COL. ROBERT SHAW, DENZEL WASHINGTON AS PVT. SILAS TRIP, MORGAN FREEMAN AS SGT. MAJ. JOHN RAWLINS

RUNNING TIME: 122 MINUTES

The historical drama *Glory* tells a story that almost certainly would be told differently today. A change in focus might have been a good thing, in that it would have seemed timelier and more progressive. But it might have been a bad thing, since the movie that was made is so well-crafted and moving.

Legend has it that Kevin Jarre got the idea for his screenplay when, while walking across the Boston Common, he noticed a Civil War memorial that included Black soldiers. That inspired him to research the story of a Massachusetts regiment composed of Black recruits led by white officers.

The regiment was led by Robert Gould Shaw (played in the film by Matthew Broderick), the son of wealthy Boston abolitionists.

After nearly being killed in combat, he is promoted to colonel and placed in charge of a Union volunteer regiment populated mostly by Northern Black free men and former slaves. That group includes Trip (Denzel Washington), a rebellious runaway slave, and John Rawlins (Morgan Freeman), a wary but pragmatic gravedigger.

Although honored by the assignment, Robert soon finds himself overwhelmed by it. Only in his twenties, he has no leadership experience and has little in common with the recruits he is commanding.

He is also naively unprepared for the racism within the Union brass, which has no intention of sending this symbolic regiment into combat and initially even denies the enlistees pay and uniforms.

Eventually, the regiment proves itself in battle, prompting Robert to volunteer his unit for a rugged assignment: storming a seemingly impregnable South Carolina fort.

The film was both an artistic and financial success, earning five Academy Award nominations.

Nearly everything about the production is first-rate, from Edward Zwick's assured direction to James Horner's stirring musical score to Freddie Francis' Oscar-winning cinematography. With a script based partially on Shaw's letters to his family, it has an authenticity lacking in most war films.

Yet there must have been times when Jarre (who died of heart failure at age fifty-six in 2011) wondered whether he should have taken a different route across the Boston Common. Not only was he excluded from the Oscar nominations, but his screenplay also was widely misunderstood and second-guessed by reviewers.

Several critics missed one of Jarre's key points: that the Black enlistees really did not need callow, if well-intentioned, white officers to lead them.

While acknowledging the film's virtues, legendary critic Roger Ebert was among those wondering why the story had to be told from Robert's perspective. "*Glory* is a strong and valuable film no matter whose eyes it is seen through," Ebert wrote. "But there is still, I suspect, another and quite different film to be made from the same material."

Would that have a been a better film? Perhaps.

Certainly Washington merited more screen time for his dynamic performance

> **"YOU GET TO GO BACK TO BOSTON, BIG HOUSE AND ALL THAT. WHAT ABOUT US? WHAT DO WE GET?"**
> — DENZEL WASHINGTON AS SILAS TRIP, TO MATTHEW BRODERICK AS ROBERT SHAW

as a defiant, embittered former slave who sees the war and its aftermath more clearly than the officers. His Supporting Actor Oscar accelerated his inevitable ascent to stardom.

Freeman's role as a wise but reluctant conduit between the white officers and the Black recruits foreshadowed many of his subsequent characters. Andre Braugher also does nice work as a privileged family friend of Robert who finds it difficult co-existing with his less educated, more racially conscious counterparts within the unit.

The film undoubtedly was told from Robert's perspective, in part, because Broderick was a bigger name in Hollywood in 1989 than Washington or Freeman. That would not have been the case had it been made even a couple of years later.

Even without detracting from Washington's and Freeman's stellar work, Broderick's sensitive performance is one of the film's highlights. His character radiates fear and uncertainty, but also great integrity and courage, as he attempts to transcend his shortcomings in a nearly impossible assignment.

Like many realistic war films, *Glory* is not always easy to watch. The climax (a suicidal charge on the South Carolina fort) takes some of the wind out of the audience's sails—a reaction that is not softened by the symbolic ending or a postscript stating that the experiences of that Massachusetts regiment helped trigger a greater role for Black troops in the Civil War.

A more socially conscious version of *Glory* might well have been emotionally rich and educational. That description, however, also applies to the film that was made. ■

GOODFELLAS

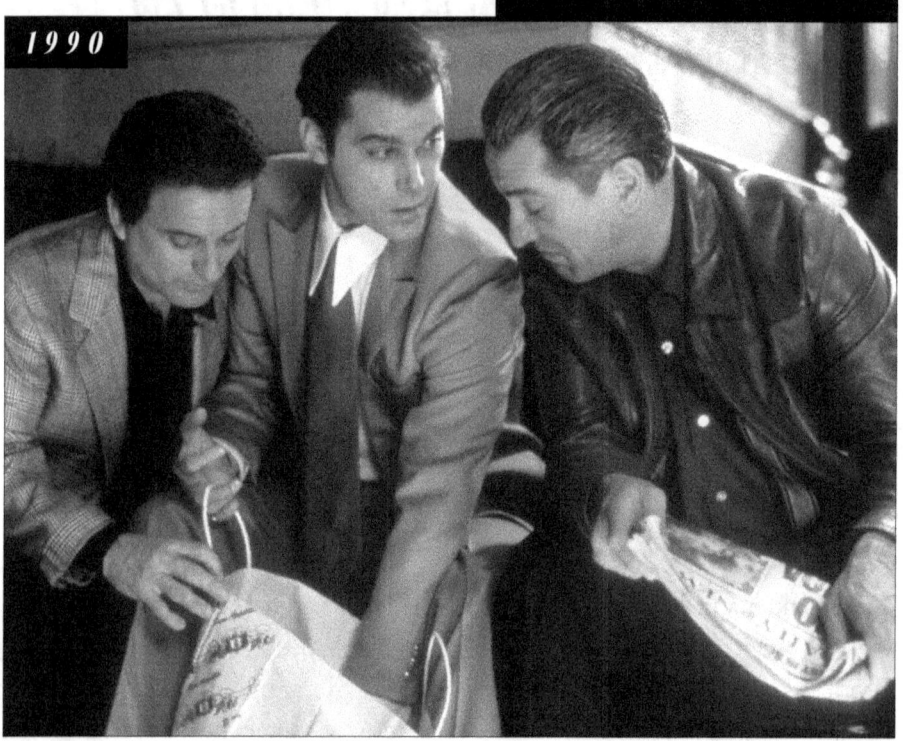

1990

DIRECTOR: MARTIN SCORSESE

PRODUCER: IRWIN WINKLER

SCREENPLAY: NICHOLAS PILEGGI AND MARTIN SCORSESE, BASED ON PILEGGI'S BOOK *WISEGUY*

STARRING: ROBERT DE NIRO AS JIMMY CONWAY, RAY LIOTTA AS HENRY HILL, JOE PESCI AS TOMMY DEVITO

RUNNING TIME: 146 MINUTES

A violent, profane look at crime in New York, *GoodFellas* could be seen as a typical Martin Scorsese film. What elevates it above most of the legendary director's other crime dramas is that it also is instructive.

Many mob movies depict the protagonist as a victim of circumstance, or someone who simply makes bad choices. Henry Hill, the central character in *GoodFellas* (played as an adult by Ray Liotta), is not like that. He's a kid attracted by the lifestyle and perks enjoyed by the mobsters in his neighborhood. As he says in a voiceover near the beginning of the film, "Being a gangster was better than being the president of the United States."

The seductive but ultimately perilous lifestyle of gangland figures is amply documented in the screenplay, adapted by Scorsese and Nicholas Pileggi from Pileggi's nonfiction book *Wiseguy*. In a much-celebrated uninterrupted tracking shot, for example, Henry avoids a crowd scene outside the Copacabana nightclub by escorting his future wife through the club's basement and kitchen to a ringside table near the stage.

Henry begins running errands for the mob at age thirteen and quickly rises in importance by accepting two critical rules of the fraternity: Never rat on your friends, and always keep your mouth shut. (Both rules eventually are broken, but not for a long time nor without provocation.)

Small wonder that Scorsese uses Tony Bennett's recording of "Rags to Riches" to play over the opening credits.

Henry forms particular friendships with two gang members. Jimmy Conway (played by Robert De Niro) is a natural leader who is capable of murder but prefers robbery. The wisecracking but volatile Tommy DeVito (Joe Pesci) can be the life of the party one moment and a cold-blooded killer the next. Veteran character actor Paul Sorvino has a small but pivotal role as the pragmatic neighborhood gangland chief, who is so cautious about bugging that he does not own a telephone.

At first, Henry's life appears too good to be true. The gangsters commit a series of crimes with few repercussions. Even in prison, they are treated like kings.

As Henry tells his skeptical bride-to-be (Lorraine Bracco, nine years before she co-starred in television's ultimate crime drama, *The Sopranos*), you have to be an idiot to get caught. But these men are not rocket scientists, and all eventually pay a steep price for their transgressions.

Scorsese tells his episodic story largely through flashbacks and voiceovers. While valuable in providing transition, these devices are perhaps a trifle overdone—and would all but sink Scorsese's less successful semi-sequel, *Casino*, five years later.

On the whole, however, this is a remarkably assured piece of storytelling that, according to the book *Based on a True Story* by Jonathan Vankin and John Whalen, is all the more powerful for being essentially factual.

Henry is portrayed as a loyalist who dutifully follows orders but is not bright or bloodthirsty enough for a leadership role. Although he pistol-whips a neighbor

> ## "AS FAR BACK AS I REMEMBER, I ALWAYS WANTED TO BE A GANGSTER."
> — RAY LIOTTA AS HENRY HILL

who makes unwanted advances on his girlfriend and is an accessory to several murders, he never actually kills anyone.

This should have been a star-making performance for Liotta, who plays Henry with the right mixture of bravado and dimwitted naivete. But, although it led to some prominent roles in the early 1990s (including an unconvincingly eloquent Shoeless Joe Jackson in *Field of Dreams*), by 1999, he was playing a security guard in *Muppets from Space*.

The film proved a better career vehicle for Pesci, who deservedly won a Supporting Actor Academy Award as the fatally insecure Tommy. Bracco also received a nomination.

De Niro initially appears to be walking through a role unworthy of his talent (this being a decade before he began routinely accepting roles in witless comedies unworthy of his talent). By the final hour, however, his character becomes more substantial as he is transformed into a man whose loyalty to his friends is superseded by greed, paranoia, and an instinct for survival.

The film's closing scenes are poignant. After testifying against his partners in crime, Henry is relocated via the federal witness protection program. This might have been seen as a triumph in a standard crime drama. But, as Henry sadly notes, "I have to wait around like everybody else."

He also learned that anyone who goes from rags to riches also can descend from riches to rags. ■

THE GREAT ESCAPE

1963

DIRECTOR: JOHN STURGES

PRODUCER: JOHN STURGES

SCREENPLAY: JAMES CLAVELL AND W.R. BURNETT, BASED ON THE BOOK BY PAUL BRICKHILL

STARRING: STEVE MCQUEEN AS CAPT. VIRGIL HILTS, JAMES GARNER AS LT. BOB HENDLEY

RUNNING TIME: 168 MINUTES

There are a lot of reasons *The Great Escape* should not have risen to classic-movie status. It's nearly three hours long. Its claim to authenticity is exaggerated. And there's also the matter of the ending.

"What kind of escape is this?" legendary producer Samuel Goldwyn once asked. "Nobody gets out."

That is not exactly true. Suffice it to say, however, that the mission is not an unqualified success.

Still, the 1963 prison-camp saga is widely regarded by audiences and critics alike as one of the greatest of action-adventure films. It owes that status to a compelling story enacted by a top ensemble cast and orchestrated by a filmmaker who rarely received his due.

The story is based on a true episode during World War II. Distracted from the war effort by a series of POW escapes, the German high command elects to confine all of the escape artists to a single, heavily fortified, and isolated camp, "putting all the rotten eggs in one basket," as the commandant tells one prisoner.

The fundamental flaw of that logic is soon demonstrated, as British officer Roger Bartlett (played by Richard Attenborough) begins organizing the other POWs in a mass-escape plan that involves simultaneously constructing three tunnels and forging identification and travel documents.

His accomplices include a rebellious American motorcycle buff (Steve McQueen), an American flier with a considerable talent for con artistry (James Garner), and a claustrophobic Polish ex-coal miner (Charles Bronson). Other familiar actors in the cast include James Coburn and David McCallum.

While acknowledging that some of the characters are composites, a prologue insists that every incident in the film is true.

Not quite. There were no Americans in the actual camp, and the two most famous scenes—McQueen's character jumping a barbed-wire fence on a motorcycle and Garner's character attempting to fly a stolen plane to safety—never happened.

This film made McQueen a star and solidified Garner's screen persona (first developed in television's *Maverick*) as a charming guy with a streak of larceny in his soul. Bronson gives his finest film performance, although in his case the bar is set pretty low. Attenborough, often cast as a wimp, is excellent in a more forceful role.

Considerable credit belongs to producer-director John Sturges not only for the spot-on casting, but also for holding the production together. This must have been a difficult movie to make.

Garner was threatened with deportation during filming in Germany for supporting protesters in a Munich demonstration. Bronson did his part for cast morale by calmly informing McCallum that he was going to steal his wife at the time, actress Jill Ireland—and making good on the threat. (Bronson and Ireland later married and were still together at the time of her death in 1990.)

Upset over the size of his role and his motivation for certain actions, McQueen briefly left the production until concessions were made. That prompted Garner, years later, to utter the classic quote, "Steve wanted to play the hero, but he didn't want to do anything heroic."

> **"I HAVEN'T SEEN BERLIN YET, FROM THE GROUND OR FROM THE AIR, AND I PLAN TO DO BOTH BEFORE THE WAR IS OVER."**
> — STEVE MCQUEEN AS VIRGIL HILTS

For that matter, it took Sturges ten years to convince a studio to bankroll the project.

Sturges is seldom ranked among the top filmmakers of his era, probably due to a series of late-career box-office flops. At his best, however, he was a master of directing what might be termed intelligent action-adventure films, such as *Bad Day at Black Rock*, *Gunfight at the OK Corral*, and *The Magnificent Seven*.

Despite its running time, *The Great Escape* is paced so well that it never seems inordinately long. It also features fully developed characters—a rarity in the action-adventure genre.

If nothing else, Sturges and screenwriters James Clavell and W.R. Burnett deserved considerable credit merely for the way they handled the ending. They use Elmer Bernstein's rousing theme music and a baseball, as a symbol of defiance, to transform a potentially downbeat climax into a tribute to the indomitable Allied spirit.

Displaying the type of courage few filmmakers possess, Sturges arranged for a special screening of the movie in Great Britain to survivors of the actual escape. Despite the historical liberties that were taken, he reportedly was rewarded with a standing ovation.

That was a telling endorsement from a group of veterans who might not have wanted to do anything heroic, but were heroes nonetheless. ∎

I CONFESS

1953

DIRECTOR: ALFRED HITCHCOCK

PRODUCER: ALFRED HITCHCOCK

SCREENPLAY: GEORGE TABORI AND WILLIAM ARCHIBALD FROM THE PLAY *NOS DEUX CONSCIENCES* BY PAUL ANTHELME

STARRING: MONTGOMERY CLIFT AS FATHER MICHAEL LOGAN, ANNE BAXTER AS RUTH GRANDFORT

RUNNING TIME: 95 MINUTES

One of Alfred Hitchcock's favorite themes was that of a virtuous man being accused of a crime with no easy way of proving his innocence.

Ironically, the director's two most specific examinations of this topic (the 1953 drama *I Confess* and 1957's *The Wrong Man*) were critical and box-office disappointments.

Despite the odd casting of fifty-two-year-old Henry Fonda as a thirty-eight-year-old Italian American musician and an unwise decision to utilize a semi-documentary form, *The Wrong Man* at least rises to midlevel Hitchcock.

Although handsomely filmed and boasting a top-notch cast, *I Confess* falls short of even that standard. Years later, Hitchcock was seemingly clueless to identify the cause.

At first glance, the plot seems tailor-made for the director. Father Michael Logan (played by Montgomery Clift) is a young Canadian priest serving a parish in Quebec City. One night, he is summoned to hear a shocking confession: Parish caretaker Otto Keller (O.E. Hasse) admits to killing the owner of a nearby house in the course of robbing it.

Bound by the sanctity of the confessional, Father Michael cannot reveal what he knows to the police. That becomes particularly sticky when the priest himself becomes a suspect in the murder.

Those suspicions are not entirely unfounded. The caretaker disguised himself by wearing a hassock, and witnesses spotted him in that garb as he left the scene of the crime.

In addition, Father Michael had an apparent motive: The murder victim (an unsavory attorney) had been blackmailing Ruth Grandfort, a pre-priesthood girlfriend of Michael.

Ruth had entered a loveless marriage with a Quebec politician when she feared Michael had been killed in World War II. When he returned from overseas, she set up a rendezvous with Michael (without informing him she was married). The two were caught in a compromising situation on property the attorney owned.

With the evidence against him mounting, Father Michael's only apparent means of saving himself from the gallows would be to divulge the confession while on trial for murder.

In an interview with Peter Bogdanovich for the book *Who the Devil Made It: Conversations with Legendary Film Directors,* Hitchcock attributed the film's failure to conflicts with Clift and what he considered the miscasting of Anne Baxter as Ruth.

Swedish actress Anita Bjork, Hitch's original choice for Ruth, was sacked by the Warner Brothers studio when she arrived in Canada with a lover and an illegitimate child in tow. This was an era in which even a star of Ingrid Bergman's magnitude was blackballed in the United States under similar circumstances.

The acting, however, is the least of Hitchcock's problems here. Although his Method acting training clashed with the director's highly structured stye, Clift

> ## "HE CAN'T TELL (POLICE) WHAT HE HEARD IN CONFESSION."
> — O.E. HASSE AS OTTO KELLER

gives a typically strong performance. Baxter might not resemble Hitchcock's standard femme fatale, but she's at least adequate in the role.

They are backed by a solid supporting cast that includes Karl Malden as the dogged police detective, Brian Aherne as the conflicted prosecutor, and Dolly Haas as the caretaker's conscience-stricken wife. The location filming in Quebec is outstanding.

Hitchcock, however, is unable to transcend the weaknesses in the screenplay, which was adapted by George Tabori and William Archibald from a French play. Much of the story is told in flashbacks, a device that Hitch seldom used well.

In addition, Ruth and Otto are erratically characterized. She treats her husband sometimes with affectionate respect, but sometimes with inexplicable cruelty. The caretaker, meanwhile, is transformed from a frightened German immigrant grateful to Father Michael for past kindnesses to a bitter, taunting monster who all but dares the priest to turn him in.

The play concluded with Michael convicted and hanged before the truth could be revealed. Undoubtedly under pressure from the studio and censors, Hitchcock nixed that ending. But his alternative, which features an improbable shooting and chase scene, is one of the weakest climaxes to any of his films.

An original poster for *I Confess* posed the question, "If you knew what he knew, what would you do?"

But most filmgoers are not Catholic priests. Father Michael essentially had two choices: remain silent or leave the priesthood. There is no indication in either the story or Clift's portrayal that the character ever considered forsaking his vows.

That, in a nutshell, represents the problem with *I Confess*. Hitchcock is working with an intriguing concept, but one that does not generate a lot of suspense. And the legendary director was never known as the Master of Moral Dilemmas. ∎

JOHNNY TREMAIN

1957

DIRECTOR: ROBERT STEVENSON

PRODUCER: WALT DISNEY

SCREENPLAY: ESTHER FORBES AND TOM BLACKBURN FROM FORBES' NOVEL

STARRING: HAL STALMASTER AS JOHNNY TREMAIN, LUANA PATTEN AS PRISCILLA LAPHAM

RUNNING TIME: 80 MINUTES

What are the two things that *Saving Private Ryan*, *All Quiet on the Western Front*, *M*A*S*H*, and *Platoon* have in common?

All, of course, are acclaimed movies that focus on wars. And none of them covers the Revolutionary War.

Despite the obvious dramatic potential, the war for America's independence has spawned remarkably few quality films.

Director John Ford's *Drums Along the Mohawk* has the best reputation, but I always have considered it more about a colonial family's struggles against the backdrop of the war than an account of the actual conflict.

Such other Revolutionary-era films as *The Devil's Disciple,* Mel Gibson's *The Patriot,* and the musical *1776* were critical and/or box-office disappointments.

An unpretentious Disney film intended primarily for children might top them all in explaining the roots of the conflict.

Based on Esther Forbes' novel, *Johnny Tremain* originally was intended as a two-part episode on Walt Disney's weekly television program. But Disney was impressed enough by the rushes that he transformed it into a big-screen release.

Set in Boston during the 1770s, it views the revolution through the eyes of the titular fictional character, a teenaged silversmith's apprentice.

Left without a trade after badly burning his hand in an accident, Johnny falls in with a rebellious youth group, the Sons of Liberty. His cohorts in the group include his former employer's granddaughter, Priscilla Lapham (who becomes his girlfriend), and a slightly older teen, Rab, who is the rebel force's unofficial leader.

Johnny meets such historical figures as Paul Revere and Sam Adams, participates in the Boston Tea Party, witnesses Revere's midnight ride, and eventually fights the British in the battles of Lexington and Concord.

This is History 101 for youths, and serious students of the American Revolution likely will find this movie hopelessly elementary. But the filmmakers do provide a clean storyline and a remarkably even-handed treatment of the opposing forces.

Nearly all Revolutionary War films depict the British as fools or sadists. There are a couple of fools in *Johnny Tremain* and at least one outright villain—a foppish Tory merchant played by Sebastian Cabot (without his trademark beard).

For the most part, however, the British military leaders are portrayed as reasonable enough men who are unhappily following orders from an absentee government. Had it been made twenty years later, the film might have been seen as a parable for Vietnam—although the deeply conservative Disney undoubtedly would have been appalled by such a comparison.

It might not be a coincidence that a Brit, Robert Stevenson, directed this film. He was behind the cameras for many of Disney's top-grossing films over the next decade, including *Mary Poppins.*

Two other studio regulars, composer George Bruns and screenwriter-lyricist Tom Blackburn, joined forces for a catchy tune, "The Liberty Tree." It is sung by the patriots in the aftermath of the Boston Tea Party, presumably

> "THERE IS A TIME FOR CASTING SILVER AND A TIME FOR CASTING CANNON. IF THAT ISN'T IN THE HOLY WRIT, IT SHOULD BE."
> — WALTER SANDE AS PAUL REVERE

mesmerizing British troops to the extent that they preferred humming along instead of making arrests.

Disney did not exactly bust his budget on high-priced sets or actors. The film is shot almost entirely on soundstages. The cast is populated by such competent but low-voltage character actors as Cabot, Walter Sande, and Jeff York.

For the juvenile leads, Disney tapped former child actress Luana Patten to play Priscilla and future *West Side Story* co-star Richard Beymer (billed here as Dick Beymer) for Rab.

As Johnny, seventeen-year-old Hal Stalmaster was plucked from obscurity — and, despite a solid performance, quickly returned to it. He wound up leaving acting a decade later.

The film ends with the Battle of Concord, but its truest scene occurs moments earlier.

After both sides are warned against initiating hostilities at Lexington, a shot rings out to trigger the warfare. Asked by an underling who fired first, a British general glumly replies, "One of them, one of us. What difference does it make?"

It is a shame Disney died before turning his attention to the War of 1812. Now there is a war that has really been underrepresented in cinematic history. ∎

KISS OF DEATH

1947

DIRECTOR: HENRY HATHAWAY

PRODUCER: FRED KOHLMAR

SCREENPLAY: BEN HECHT AND CHARLES LEDERER FROM A STORY BY ELEAZAR LIPSKY

STARRING: VICTOR MATURE AS NICK BIANCO, RICHARD WIDMARK AS TOMMY UDO

RUNNING TIME: 98 MINUTES

The gritty crime drama *Kiss of Death* is best remembered for Richard Widmark's electrifying screen debut as the giggling, psychotic hoodlum Tommy Udo.

This is a far better film than the disappointing Nicolas Cage-David Caruso 1995 remake. It is well-written by Ben Hecht and Charles Lederer, and tautly directed by Henry Hathaway, also featuring underrated performances by Victor Mature and Coleen Gray as the nominal leads.

But it could have been a great movie had it not been constricted by censorship and the social mores of the era.

Mature plays Nick Bianco, a down-on-his-luck ex-con who orchestrates a jewelry store robbery in a New York skyscraper on Christmas Eve. Apprehended for the crime, he refuses to rat on his partners when offered a deal by assistant district attorney Louis D'Angelo (Brian Donlevy)—an attitude that initially earns the admiration of gangland hit man Tommy.

Nick undergoes a change of heart in prison after his wife is violated by one of his erstwhile partners and eventually commits suicide, forcing the couple's beloved daughters into an orphanage.

By agreeing to inform, he is able to earn parole, land a respectable job in a brickyard, and start a new life with his daughters and an adoring former baby-sitter (Gray), whom he marries.

But his second chance at happiness is jeopardized when he testifies against Tommy in a murder case—and the crazed mobster seeks revenge after beating the rap.

Although he later became better known for such Westerns as the John Wayne version of *True Grit,* Hathaway was at the time a specialist in directing the semi-documentary dramas that became a fixture of the 20th Century Fox studio in the late 1940s. He enhances this film's atmosphere by shooting in actual New York locations (including the Sing Sing Prison) and does a terrific job of ratcheting up the tension.

Yet even filmgoers who believe contemporary directors such as Martin Scorsese overdose on violence and profanity might concede that *Kiss of Death* goes too far in the other direction.

When censors nixed scenes depicting the sexual assault and suicide of Nick's first wife, the actress portraying her (Patricia Morison) had her entire role cut from the picture. Attempting to goad Tommy into violence near the end of the film, Nick cannot come up with a more volatile taunt than, "Beat it. Peddle your papers. Go on, blow"—then asserts in a telephone conversation with Louis that he needled Tommy pretty hard. And the bloody final confrontation ends improbably with all parties still alive, reportedly because studio executives changed the original ending.

Known more for his beefcake appearance (his nickname was "The Hunk") than his acting talent, Mature gives a surprisingly affecting performance as a man whose contempt for law enforcement is outweighed by his devotion to his family.

> **"YOU KNOW WHAT I DO TO SQUEALERS? I LET THEM HAVE IT IN THE BELLY, SO THEY CAN ROLL AROUND FOR A LONG TIME THINKING IT OVER."**
> — RICHARD WIDMARK AS TOMMY UDO

Gray inspired few comparisons to Meryl Streep in a long career that ended primarily in television guest-starring roles. But as she demonstrated in playing opposite Tyrone Power in *Nightmare Alley,* John Payne in *Kansas City Confidential,* and even in a one-scene role with John Wayne in *Red River,* she could portray a woman in love as convincingly as any actress of the era. She radiates such adoration in her first scene with Mature that it is not necessary for Hathaway to spend a lot of time detailing the progression of their relationship.

Still, there is little doubt that Widmark steals the picture in his first big-screen appearance. His Udo would rank high on any list of sadistic, scum-of-the-earth movie villains.

The character famously pushes a wheelchair-bound woman (played by acclaimed stage actress Mildred Dunnock) down a flight of stairs, expresses a preference for shooting victims in the stomach so they can writhe in pain before expiring, and gives a girlfriend her walking papers so he can go nightclub-hopping with Nick. His laugh seems to well up involuntarily from the depth of Hades.

Widmark received an Academy Award nomination—but, in a classic example of how the Supporting Actor category takes all kinds, he lost to Santa Claus (Edmund Gwenn in *Miracle on 34th Street*).

While Widmark later made a conscious effort to avoid typecasting as a sociopath, even his more sympathetic characters were seldom particularly likable. In the 1953 film noir classic *Pickup on South Street,* for example, he punches out the heroine, revives her by pouring a bottle of beer over her head, and then passionately kisses her. And he was supposedly the hero (or anti-hero) of that film.

Although Widmark earned acclaim for that and many other performances in a 45-year film career, he never received another Oscar nomination.

He might have been tempted to tell Academy members to go peddle their papers. ■

A LEAGUE OF THEIR OWN

1992

DIRECTOR: PENNY MARSHALL

PRODUCERS: ELLIOT ABBOTT AND ROBERT GREENHUT

SCREENPLAY: LOWELL GANZ AND BABALOO MANDEL FROM A STORY BY KIM WILSON AND KELLY CANDAELE

STARRING: TOM HANKS AS JIMMY DUGAN, GEENA DAVIS AS DOTTIE HINSON

RUNNING TIME: 128 MINUTES

Baseball buffs found it an authentic and educational glimpse at an often-overlooked chapter of the game's history. But you do not need to be a sports fan to enjoy the 1992 baseball comedy *A League of Their Own*.

Although the characters are fictionalized, director Penny Marshall and screenwriters Lowell Ganz and Babaloo Mandel stick pretty close to the facts about the development of the World War II-era All-American League.

Amid fears that the wholesale drafting of standout players would prevent men's Major League Baseball from surviving the war, millionaire candy manufacturer Walter Harvey (a thinly disguised doppelganger for chewing-gum magnate and Chicago Cubs owner Phil Wrigley) forms the women's league in 1943.

Searching for talent, a veteran scout (played by a funny Jon Lovitz) finds a hot prospect in catcher Dottie Hinson (Geena Davis), who is playing sandlot ball in Oregon.

Content to work on a family-owned farm while awaiting the return of her serviceman husband, Dottie is not interested in joining the new league. But her less talented, insecure younger sister Kit Keller (Lori Petty) has her heart set on playing. Dottie relents when the scout agrees to take them as a package deal.

The sisters are assigned to the Rockford (Illinois) Peaches, one of only four franchises in the Midwest-based league. They are managed by Jimmy Dugan (Tom Hanks), a former major-league slugger who has descended into alcoholism.

Jimmy is so soused at the outset of the season that he shirks the bulk of his managerial duties, but his attitude changes as the league begins catching on.

Experienced filmgoers might think they know where this story is going. The season, they believe, will end with a climactic confrontation between the sisters (one of whom is traded to a rival team). There is also an expectation that Dottie's husband will be killed in combat, clearing the way for her to fall in love with the boozy but endearing Jimmy.

The on-field action unfolds predictably, and some Columbia Pictures executives also favored a Dottie-Jimmy romantic subplot. Indeed, a scene originally was written in which the manager makes a pass at his star player.

Marshall wisely discarded that scene, replacing it with one in which Dottie's husband (Bill Pullman, in a cameo role), after being wounded in action, surprises her by arriving unannounced at the team hotel. That reunion is so poignantly filmed that some viewers undoubtedly hated themselves for hoping that this obviously loving couple would be separated.

This was clearly a labor of love for Marshall, who put the cast through several months of baseball training in a successful attempt to make the action scenes convincing.

Davis landed the role of Dottie after original choice Debra Winger bowed out over creative differences with Marshall, which reportedly included Winger's objection to the casting of Madonna as one of the ballplayers.

"THERE'S NO CRYING IN BASEBALL!"
— TOM HANKS AS JIMMY DUGAN

While the screenplay takes some dramatic license (contrary to what the film depicts, the league was popular from the beginning), the filmmakers get a surprising amount of detail right. League officials did require their players to attend charm school, for example, and the league's public relations man eventually did take over the entire operation.

Dugan's character was based on Jimmie Foxx, a Hall of Fame first baseman who managed a team in the All-American League while fighting what ultimately proved to be a losing battle with the bottle.

While Foxx more closely resembled Brian Dennehy than Tom Hanks, the latter expertly blends humor and pathos in what, despite his top billing, is actually a glorified supporting role. He did, of course, deliver the film's most memorable line: "There's no crying in baseball!"

Made only two years after he starred in the notorious flop *The Bonfire of the Vanities,* this movie reignited Hanks' career and helped propel him to eventual superstardom.

As for Davis, her experience with this film sparked a highly unorthodox avocation.

Although she had no athletic background at the time, the tall, graceful actress easily passed for a ballplayer—and her understated acting style dovetailed nicely with her character's career ambivalence. Off-set, she soon became an enthusiastic proponent of the federal Title IX gender-equity regulations for high school and college athletics.

And, five years after the film was made, Davis took up archery. She became proficient enough at the sport to qualify for the semifinals of the 2000 U.S. Olympic Trials—finishing 24th in a field of 300.

Although she never tasted Olympic glory, Davis did not express much disappointment. She undoubtedly realized there is no crying in archery. ■

THE LEMON DROP KID

1951

DIRECTORS: SIDNEY LANFIELD AND FRANK TASHLIN

PRODUCER: ROBERT WELCH

SCREENPLAY: FRANK TASHLIN, EDMUND HARTMANN, ROBERT O'BRIEN, AND IRVING ELINSON, FROM A STORY BY DAMON RUNYON AND EDMUND BELOIN

STARRING: BOB HOPE AS THE LEMON DROP KID, MARILYN MAXWELL AS BRAINEY BAXTER

RUNNING TIME: 91 MINUTES

For nearly a decade beginning in 1943, Bob Hope annually ranked among the top 10 box-office attractions in movies. But, aside from his assorted road trips with Bing Crosby, few of his big-screen comedies are well-regarded today.

There are multiple reasons for this critical transformation. Hope was less popular among baby boomers than audiences of his own generation, no doubt in part due to his unswerving support of the Vietnam War. And even in his better films, he tended to play the same character: a wisecracking coward who hides his insecurities behind a veneer of bravado.

One reason the Hope-Crosby road pictures still work is that they forced Hope into a slightly different type of role: a good-hearted schnook constantly outwitted by his smarter, more charismatic pal. Crosby also needed Hope's zaniness to enliven his laid-back, somewhat remote screen image.

Even his admirers concede that Hope's later films were pretty sorry affairs. And his previously pristine public image took a hit from unauthorized biographies that depicted him as demanding behind the scenes and frequently unfaithful to his wife of 69 years.

Ironically, the latter two traits helped make *The Lemon Drop Kid* one of Hope's better big-screen efforts.

The film also benefits from the introduction of a classic holiday song that today's audiences seldom associate with this movie or its star.

Hope plays the title role (when addressed in court by his real name, he does not recognize it), so named because of his fondness for lemon drop candies.

As the film opens, the Kid is running a racetrack scam in Florida. His victims include the mistress of gangster Moose Malloy, costing the latter $10,000 in winnings. Moose (played by Fred Clark) wants the debt repaid by Christmas Eve—or else.

Observing the effectiveness that charitable organizations have in raising funds around the holidays, the Kid hatches a plan once he returns to New York. Enlisting his nightclub entertainer girlfriend, Brainey Baxter (Marilyn Maxwell), and their Broadway pals as accomplices, he obtains a city license to collect money to build a retirement home for elderly women on the site of Moose's abandoned casino.

Although Brainey and the Kid's other cohorts are unaware of his motives, he plans to pocket enough of the money to square himself with Moose and leave "the old dolls" (in his words) literally out in the cold.

The initial success of this venture, however, attracts the attention of Brainey's employer, unsavory nightclub operator Oxford Charlie (Lloyd Nolan), who wants to muscle in on the action.

That sets up a frenetic climax in which the Kid tries to escape the clutches of the rival gangsters while belatedly attempting to do the right thing for the elderly women.

The movie is based on a Damon Runyon story filmed in 1934. Never a versatile actor, Hope shaped the material around his standard screen persona, but at least he was working with edgier material than was his custom.

> ## *"I'M TURNING OVER A NEW LEAF. I'LL NEVER BE CAUGHT AGAIN."*
> — BOB HOPE AS THE LEMON DROP KID

While former band singer Maxwell brings an appropriately brassy quality to her role, it was evidently an open secret at the time that she owed her casting to a steamy off-camera affair with Hope. In any event, the chemistry between the co-stars was evident, and the love scenes were unusually intense for a Hope movie.

Upon learning of the holiday setting, Hope insisted upon the creation of a Christmas-themed song.

Although few such holiday tunes in the past seventy years have gained widespread public acceptance, the Academy Award-winning composing team of Ray Evans and Jay Livingston pulled it off. Their collaboration, "Silver Bells," quickly developed into one of the beloved standards of the season, although it was stunningly overlooked in that year's Oscar nominations for Best Song.

Hope, however, was dissatisfied with the original presentation and demanded retakes, directed by screenwriter Frank Tashlin, several months after the remainder of the film had been completed.

Sidney Lanfield, who directed the rest of the film, was infuriated by the change and never worked with Hope again—but the eventual four-minute scene in which Maxwell and Hope perform the song while strolling down a snowy street is one of the film's highlights.

Hope's attempts to gain the same identification with "Silver Bells" as Crosby did with "White Christmas" fell flat, however. Although he performed the song with various female co-stars on his annual television Christmas specials, few viewers were aware of its origins.

By the time Hope and Maxwell got around to recording "Silver Bells," other singers had beaten them to it. In a case of life imitating art, the best-selling version was recorded by Bing Crosby. ∎

A LETTER TO THREE WIVES

1949

DIRECTOR: JOSEPH L. MANKIEWICZ

PRODUCER: SOL SIEGEL

SCREENPLAY: JOSEPH L. MANKIEWICZ AND VERA CASPARY FROM THE MAGAZINE SERIAL *A LETTER TO FIVE WIVES* BY JOHN KLEMPNER

STARRING: JEANNE CRAIN AS DEBORAH BISHOP, ANN SOTHERN AS RITA PHIPPS, LINDA DARNELL AS LORA MAE HOLLINGSWAY

RUNNING TIME: 103 MINUTES

In title and plot, *A Letter to Three Wives* could be described as a "chick flick."

Actually, however, the comedy-drama appeals to all audiences—a tribute to its smart, witty screenplay and unorthodox casting that, for the most part, works.

The film opens with three longtime friends waiting to chaperone underprivileged children on a river cruise. As the women are about to board, they are handed a telegram from town seductress Addie Ross informing them that she's leaving town—and taking one of their husbands with her.

Since all of the husbands have some history with Addie, each of the wives has cause for concern. Because cellphones did not exist at the time, they have little recourse but to wait for the cruise to end before attempting to discover the truth.

The three parallel stories are told primarily in flashback.

Former Navy nurse Deborah Bishop (played by Jeanne Crain) hails from a poor background and feels out of place in the social circle of her wealthy husband, Brad (Jeffrey Lynn).

Rita Phipps (Ann Sothern) has built a solid career as a writer of radio soap operas. But her success has put her at odds with her schoolteacher husband, George (a prestardom Kirk Douglas), who views radio soaps with contempt.

Lora Mae Hollingsway (Linda Darnell) is married to her ex-boss, Porter (Paul Douglas), the well-heeled owner of a department store chain. The couple constantly bickers, fueling the insecure Porter's view that Lora Mae might simply be positioning herself for a high-priced divorce settlement.

For a variety of reasons, the segment on the Bishops never takes shape. Class distinctions probably were more important in the 1940s than today.

In the *Cosmopolitan* magazine serial that inspired the movie, Deborah was depicted as plain and socially awkward. Crain, one of the most glamorous actresses of the era, fits neither description. It does not help that Brad's character is a virtual cipher in the final version of the screenplay.

The other performers fare better. Comedy veteran Sothern is well-suited to her role as a sharp-witted career woman. Considering his subsequent image as a tough guy, Kirk Douglas seems a strange choice to portray an erudite, somewhat snobbish English teacher, but he plays the part with the requisite intelligence.

Best of all is the saga of the battling Hollingsways. Raised on literally the wrong side of the tracks (her family's modest home shakes whenever a train passes), the tough-minded Lora Mae cynically sees her infatuated boss as her ticket to a better lifestyle. Although the production code of the era prevented the filmmakers from spelling it out, she obviously withheld sex until after the marriage vows were exchanged.

The sultry Darnell, then in her late twenties, and the rough-hewn Paul Douglas, making his film debut at the age of forty-two, seem an unlikely couple. That, however, is sort of the point of their relationship. Less predictably, they also generate a feisty type of chemistry that makes it believable that love could exist beneath the contentious surface.

> **"WHY IS IT SOONER OR LATER, NO MATTER WHAT WE TALK ABOUT, WE WIND UP TALKING ABOUT ADDIE ROSS?"**
> — JEANNE CRAIN AS DEBORAH BISHOP

The supporting cast includes scene-stealing Thelma Ritter (as a friend of Lora Mae's mother) and Celeste Holm, who provides the voice of the never-seen Addie Ross.

Darnell, Sothern, and Paul Douglas easily could have earned Academy Award nominations. Perhaps because of the blurring of lines between lead and supporting roles, however, the film received no acting nods.

But writer and director Joseph L. Mankiewicz earned Oscars in both categories—a feat he repeated a year later for *All About Eve*.

The writing award was particularly merited in view of the challenges he faced in adapting the story.

The *Cosmopolitan* magazine serial included five wives (demonstrating, if nothing else, that Addie really got around). After summarily dropping one couple, Mankiewicz discovered that the screenplay still was running too long. At the behest of 20th Century Fox studio chief Darryl F. Zanuck, he eliminated another wife, even though Anne Baxter already had been cast in the role.

Perhaps more impressively, Mankiewicz infuses what could have been a soapish plot with a liberal dose of humor, much of it supplied by Sothern, Ritter, and Paul Douglas.

Mankiewicz also changed the identity of the straying husband, a decision that drew mixed reviews.

In an otherwise favorable review of the movie, Oscar historian Charles Mathews called the ending "a comedown."

On the contrary, I found it unusually satisfying, largely because the character development made it seem plausible.

Even at the end, *A Letter to Three Wives* was worth delivering. ∎

MARRIED TO THE MOB

1988

DIRECTOR: JONATHAN DEMME

PRODUCERS: KENNETH UTT AND EDWARD SAXON

SCREENPLAY: BARRY STRUGATZ AND MARK BURNS

STARRING: MICHELLE PFEIFFER AS ANGELA DE MARCO, MATTHEW MODINE AS MIKE DOWNEY

RUNNING TIME: 103 MINUTES

Not many people who first watched director Martin Scorsese's 1990 crime classic *GoodFellas* would imagine that a successful comedy could be made out of essentially the same material, focusing on Lorraine Bracco's role as a Mafia wife.

Actually, such a comedy was released two years earlier. Directed by another gifted filmmaker, Jonathan Demme, *Married to the Mob* provided an important starring role for Michelle Pfeiffer. Even she, however, was overshadowed by two supporting players.

Pfeiffer plays Angela de Marco, the unhappily married wife of mob hitman Frankie "The Cucumber" de Marco (played by a prestardom Alec Baldwin).

First glimpsed unobtrusively knocking off a victim in the middle of a subway commute, "The Cucumber" is good at his job, but is himself rubbed out by mob boss Tony "The Tiger" Russo (Dean Stockwell) when he takes an interest in the married mobster's mistress.

Angela wanted out of the marriage ("Everything has blood on it," she wails to her husband). But that does not mean she welcomes the attentions of the compulsively womanizing Tony, who makes a play for her at the funeral reception.

Accompanied by her young son, Angela attempts to start from scratch while living in a fleabag apartment on New York's Lower East Side. Tony, though, soon discovers her whereabouts—as does his insanely jealous wife, Connie (Mercedes Ruehl).

Meanwhile, young FBI agent Mike Downey (Matthew Modine), tailing the widow in hopes of using her to obtain information for a case against Tony, inevitably winds up falling in love with her.

This material is not inherently funny. As he demonstrated in such films as *Melvin and Howard* and *Something Wild*, however, Demme has a knack for putting a loopy comic spin on unusual situations.

Two of the best scenes in this film involve Angela being menaced by other mob wives in the aisle of a neighborhood supermarket and Tony engaging in a gun battle in a burger chain's drive-thru.

With one exception, Demme does a splendid job of populating his cast with skilled comic actors—even though some of them (Joan Cusack, Nancy Travis, Oliver Platt) would make their marks later on and are largely wasted in small roles.

The exception is Modine, playing a role that the filmmakers reportedly all but begged Tom Cruise to accept.

A solid dramatic actor in such 1980s films as *Full Metal Jacket* and *Gross Anatomy*, Modine does not have much of a flair for comedy. His character is supposed to be colorful, the type who would climb out of the skylight of a moving bus and join an all-Black quartet of street singers to escape detection while maintaining his surveillance of Angela.

But he still comes off as terminally bland. What should have been Modine's funniest scene, when his character reads Tony his rights while three of the mobster's goons have their guns trained on him, could have been a classic had Cruise,

> ## "EVERYTHING HAS BLOOD ON IT."
> — MICHELLE PFEIFFER AS ANGELA DE MARCO

Tom Hanks, or even Baldwin played the role.

Modine's low-voltage presence helped Stockwell and Ruehl steal the movie.

Stockwell kept reinventing himself as an actor—going from a child star in the 1940s to a sensitive young leading man in the late 1950s to a valued character actor some thirty years later—in a fascinating career interrupted by prolonged absences from the screen while he became involved in the hippie culture and later in real estate.

His mob boss with a yen for women and fast food was miles away from the arch characters he often played. But he handled the role skillfully enough to earn several critics' awards and an Academy Award nomination as a supporting actor. He lost the Oscar, however, to another comic performance, Kevin Kline's in *A Fish Called Wanda*.

Ruehl was ignored by the Academy for this film, but her Supporting Actress Oscar for *The Fisher King* three years later might have represented at least partial recognition for that oversight.

She makes an ostensible villainess almost endearing. Many in the audience must have smiled whenever her ferociously possessive character appeared.

Pfeiffer is also very good in an atypically ethnic comic role. This was one of several films she made in the late 1980s that allowed her to surmount her glamorous image and demonstrate her acting versatility.

If she was somewhat upstaged by Stockwell and Ruehl in this movie, she made amends by stealing the spotlight from nominal lead Jeff Bridges the following year with her Oscar-nominated performance as the call girl-turned-lounge singer in *The Fabulous Baker Boys*.

As any mobster—or mob wife—can attest, it is always better to get even than to get mad. ∎

MIRACLE ON 34TH STREET

1947

DIRECTOR: GEORGE SEATON

PRODUCER: WILLIAM PERLBERG

SCREENPLAY: GEORGE SEATON, FROM A STORY BY VALENTINE DAVIES

STARRING: EDMUND GWENN AS KRIS KRINGLE, MAUREEN O'HARA AS DORIS WALKER, NATALIE WOOD AS SUSAN WALKER

RUNNING TIME: 96 MINUTES

The American Film Institute once ranked *Miracle on 34th Street* the fifth-greatest fantasy in cinematic history. It might rate even higher among holiday classics.

Not bad for a Christmas movie that premiered in June.

The normally astute 20th Century Fox studio chief Darryl F. Zanuck was so unimpressed with the original script outline that he insisted the movie be released during the summer.

The studio then downplayed the holiday theme while promoting it in previews as a family film.

Zanuck reportedly was as surprised as anyone when the film became an immediate hit that developed into one of the most beloved of all holiday movies.

It also has held up better than most Christmas movies of the era, because it blends fantasy elements with modern sensibilities.

Maureen O'Hara stars as Doris Walker, an executive with Macy's department store in New York. A single mom scarred by a divorce (a plot detail that censors wanted removed from the screenplay), she is attempting to discourage the attentions of Fred Gailey (played by John Payne), the easygoing attorney who lives in her apartment complex.

She is also raising her precocious daughter, Susan (eight-year-old Natalie Wood), to take a realistic view of the world.

Doris' organization of Macy's Thanksgiving Day Parade is jeopardized when the man hired to portray Santa Claus shows up drunk.

Enter Kris Kringle (Edmund Gwenn), an eccentric white-bearded gent who claims to be the real Saint Nick. Kris is willing to not only fill in during the parade, but also serve as the department store's Santa.

For a time, all goes well. Kris' candor in sending customers to rival stores for better bargains proves a publicity windfall for Macy's. Setting up temporary lodging in Fred's apartment, he tries to convince a skeptical Susan that he is Santa while the attorney makes progress in his courtship of Doris.

But Kris makes an enemy of the store psychologist, leading to a highly publicized sanity trial that concludes on Christmas Eve.

Writer-director George Seaton's Academy Award-winning screenplay is a bit edgier than first-time viewers might expect. Macy's executives support Kris only because he's been good for business. The trial judge fears that his rulings might jeopardize his re-election bid (although spoilsports might quibble that such an election probably would be months away).

O'Hara and Payne might not have been superstars, but they were perfectly cast—so much so that the many big-screen and television remakes usually fall short in filling their roles.

Those familiar with Wood's adult career as a glamorous leading lady will find it fun seeing her convincingly play the type of smart, somewhat cynical kid that other children might avoid.

> **"I BELIEVE, I BELIEVE. IT'S SILLY, BUT I BELIEVE."**
> — NATALIE WOOD AS SUSAN WALKER

An impressive group of character actors—including Porter Hall as the loathsome psychologist, Thelma Ritter making her film debut as a Macy's customer, Gene Lockhart as the nervous judge, and William Frawley as his cigar-puffing campaign manager—fills out the cast.

Also making his big-screen debut is future Academy Award winner Jack Albertson, in the unbilled but surprisingly pivotal role as a postal clerk who makes a decision that aids in Kris' defense.

Although he occasionally had played unsympathetic roles (including an assassin in Alfred Hitchcock's *Foreign Correspondent*) earlier in his career, veteran British character actor Gwenn established the gold standard for future screen Santas.

While it sounds apocryphal, O'Hara claimed in her autobiography that Wood believed Gwenn was Santa until she saw him without makeup at a production-ending party.

Gwenn received one of the film's three Oscars, as Best Supporting Actor. Although the actor deserved recognition, classifying Kris Kringle as a supporting role is ludicrous. He appears in the opening scene, his presence is felt in the climax, and he dominates most of what transpires in between.

Without Kris, the story would be about a tentative holiday romance between a wary career woman and an idealistic attorney.

That is the type of movie that might open—and close—in June. ∎

MURPHY'S ROMANCE

1985

DIRECTOR: MARTIN RITT

PRODUCER: LAURA ZISKIN

SCREENPLAY: IRVING RAVETCH AND HARRIET FRANK JR., FROM A NOVELLA BY MAX SCHOTT

STARRING: SALLY FIELD AS EMMA MORIARTY, JAMES GARNER AS MURPHY JONES

RUNNING TIME: 107 MINUTES

Upon first learning of the casting, I did not believe *Murphy's Romance* could possibly work. Neither, evidently, did some people at Columbia Pictures, the studio that released the romantic comedy.

James Garner at age fifty-eight and Sally Field at thirty-eight (but looking and acting even younger) did not appear to be a screen couple made in heaven. Yet the movie, like the title character, sneaks up on you and wears down your resistance.

For starters, the title is misleading. Very little screen time is devoted to actual romance. The film contains only three love scenes—and Murphy is not involved in one of those. In the most effective romantic encounter, the characters never touch.

A case also can be made that pharmacist Murphy Jones is not the primary character of the movie named for him. That might not have been the case had Columbia executives had their way on casting.

While Field and director Martin Ritt always had him in mind to play Murphy, Garner wrote in his autobiography that the studio was "adamant" that the film should be a comeback vehicle for Marlon Brando (who had not played a substantial big-screen role in nearly a decade).

Although Garner emphasized that he, Field, and Ritt were admirers of Brando, the latter two considered him wrong for this part. Coming off her second Academy Award performance (in *Places in the Heart*), Field had enough box-office clout to wield considerable influence. Her if-Garner-does-not-do-the-picture-I-do-not-do-the-picture ultimatum landed him the role.

While it is easier to imagine Brando playing Murphy than Garner portraying Vito Corleone, the right choice was made. Garner possessed the vitality, easygoing charm, and comedic skills that the role required.

In any event, the story focuses more on Field's character. She is characteristically spunky as Emma Moriarty, a financially strapped divorcee who relocates with her son (played by Corey Haim) to a small Arizona town where she hopes to start a horse ranch.

She is befriended—platonically at first—by Murphy, an opinionated, somewhat curmudgeonly but kind-hearted pharmacist who steers some business her way.

Complications soon ensue when Emma's charismatic but shiftless ex-husband, Bobby Jack (Brian Kerwin), arrives looking for a place to stay temporarily.

Emma lets him hang around for the sake of her son. But it does not take Sherlock Holmes to deduce that she eventually will be forced to make a choice between Bobby Jack and Murphy (who accompanies the family on many of its activities).

Best known for their collaborations on such gritty dramas as *Hud* and Field's first Oscar winner, *Norma Rae,* Ritt and the husband-wife screenwriting team of Irving Ravetch and Harriet Frank Jr. demonstrate a surprising flair for

> **"(IF) FRUIT HANGS ON A TREE LONG ENOUGH, IT GETS RIPE. I'M DURABLE, I'M STEADY, I'M FAITHFUL. AND I'M IN LOVE, FOR THE LAST TIME IN MY LIFE."**
> — JAMES GARNER AS MURPHY JONES

romantic comedy. The age difference between the leads is even addressed through Emma's repeated questions to Murphy about the topic.

They do, however, fall into a familiar trap for such films by resorting to what might be called The *Titanic* Syndrome (so named for the romantic triangle in the 1997 Oscar-winning melodrama)—making the third person so unworthy of the heroine's love that the audience wonders how she got involved with him in the first place.

It is not enough that Bobby Jack is depicted as an irresponsible loser. He's also shown to be a cheater in more ways than one. By the time a climactic revelation occurs, Emma's choice seems pretty obvious.

Although it received favorable reviews (and a ninety-three percent approval rating on the Rotten Tomatoes website), *Murphy's Romance* was too unpretentious to be seriously considered for year-ending awards. It did, however, provide the often-underrated Garner with his sole Oscar nomination.

The film concludes with what Garner accurately described as "one of the great love scenes," the one in which Emma and Murphy never kiss nor even touch.

They begin by discussing the weather and progress to revealing their true feelings. It works because the dialogue is moving without sounding contrived.

That even beats the idea of Marlon Brando making Sally Field an offer she couldn't refuse. ■

THE MUSIC MAN

1962

DIRECTOR: MORTON DACOSTA

PRODUCER: MORTON DACOSTA

SCREENPLAY: MARION HARGROVE, BASED ON MEREDITH WILLSON'S BROADWAY MUSICAL

STARRING: ROBERT PRESTON AS "PROFESSOR" HAROLD HILL, SHIRLEY JONES AS MARIAN PAROO

RUNNING TIME: 151 MINUTES

Thanks to surprisingly spot-on casting, great songs, and a story that would work almost as well without them, *The Music Man* is widely regarded as one of the better stage-to-screen transformations of a hit musical.

The casting part is surprising, as only a handful of the film's performers also played their roles on Broadway. Moreover, that small list included at least one more holdover than Warner Brothers studio chief Jack Warner wanted.

Despite winning a Tony Award for playing "Professor" Harold Hill on stage, Robert Preston had little reason to believe he would be asked to reprise that lead role when Warner Brothers obtained the movie rights.

Studio chief Warner was notorious for insisting that major stars headline his big-budget productions. Preston, who had played almost exclusively supporting roles (often villains) in Hollywood for more than a decade before striking gold on Broadway, hardly fit that description.

By some accounts, Warner all but begged fifty-eight-year-old Cary Grant to portray Hill on screen. Others say Frank Sinatra and Dean Martin were the leading candidates, with Gene Kelly, Danny Kaye, and Burt Lancaster also under consideration.

Kelly could have handled the part, but most of the other contenders would have been all wrong. Grant was too old and Martin too laid-back to be convincing. One could imagine Sinatra trying to fleece small-town Iowans, but much harder to believe he would have entertained second thoughts about doing so.

In any event, none of Warner's top picks showed much interest. Finally (some say at the behest of composer Meredith Willson), Preston was signed.

It proved an ideal choice. Preston was far from an accomplished singer, but his solos had been written to accommodate a limited vocal range (another reason Sinatra would not have been a good fit).

Nor, in most of his roles, was Preston a particularly charismatic actor. But he plays Hill with such energy and enthusiasm that he becomes almost a force of nature.

Only a moderately successful composer until then, Willson based *The Music Man* on his memories of growing up in Mason City, Iowa.

Harold Hill (not his real name) is a traveling salesman and second-rate con man who debarks in Mason City's fictional counterpart, River City, Iowa.

Falsely portraying himself as a music professor, Harold convinces River City residents that the arrival of a new pool table represents trouble—with a capital T and that rhymes with P and stands for pool. To ward off the juvenile delinquency that he contends billiards will foster, he proposes forming a boys band.

In reality, Harold intends to deliver only part of the goods before skipping town with most of the profits. (A first-rate con man probably would not have spent part of the money ordering band uniforms.)

His plans are complicated by attempts to expose him as a fraud—and his attraction to Marian, the skeptical librarian played by Shirley Jones.

> **"WE GOT TROUBLE, RIGHT HERE IN RIVER CITY. WITH A CAPITAL T AND THAT RHYMES WITH P AND THAT STANDS FOR POOL."**
> — SUNG BY ROBERT PRESTON AS HAROLD HILL

Preston, Pert Kelton (who played Marian's Irish mother), and the Buffalo Bills barbershop quartet were the only holdovers from the original Broadway cast.

But Jones was born to play the outwardly prim but inwardly sensual Marian. And Paul Ford was terrific as the blustering River City mayor, as was Hermione Gingold as his imperious wife.

Eight-year-old Ronny Howard seemingly lacked the singing skills to play Marian's lisping younger brother, but it really did not matter. The future television star and Oscar-winning director's hilariously tone-deaf renditions of "The Wells Fargo Wagon" and "Gary, Indiana" were so endearing that they rank among the film's highlights.

Willson wrote nearly forty songs for his original draft of the play. Nearly half of those were retained for the big-screen version. In truth, that was probably too many, as two hours and thirty-one minutes is long for a movie musical.

Those tunes, however, include the rousing "76 Trombones" and "Till There Was You," a ballad eventually recorded by such varied artists as Anita Bryant, jazz trumpeter Al Hirt and the Beatles.

The Music Man received an Academy Award nomination for Best Picture and wound up as Warner Brothers' top-grossing film of 1962. After its release, however, matters went back to status quo.

Willson spent the remainder of his stage career alternating between modest successes and outright flops. Preston returned to playing leads on Broadway and supporting roles in Hollywood.

After purchasing the screen rights to *My Fair Lady* a couple years later, Jack Warner reverted to type and bypassed stage star Julie Andrews to give the leading role of Eliza Doolittle to Audrey Hepburn.

Even Warner might have conceded, however, that the movie version of *The Music Man* might have been in trouble—with a capital T—without Robert Preston. ■

MY FAVORITE YEAR

1982

DIRECTOR: RICHARD BENJAMIN

PRODUCER: MICHAEL GRUSKOFF

SCREENPLAY: NORMAN STEINBERG AND DENNIS PALUMBO

STARRING: PETER O'TOOLE AS ALAN SWANN, MARK LINN-BAKER AS BENJY STONE

RUNNING TIME: 92 MINUTES

There are some movie roles—Rick Blaine in *Casablanca* and Norman Bates in *Psycho*, for example—that you can imagine only one actor playing.

Alan Swann, the boozy has-been actor featured in *My Favorite Year*, is not exactly one of those. There were two actors ideal for that part.

Errol Flynn, the obvious inspiration for the character, would have been one of them. But he died twenty-three years before this movie was filmed.

Thankfully for all concerned, Peter O'Toole still was around.

Alan's larger-than-life persona could be captured only by an actor with star quality, enough versatility to play both comedy and drama, a willingness to go over the top without looking foolish, and the ability to play a swashbuckler convincingly.

Jack Nicholson or Robin Williams could have fit the bill in the first three categories, but not the fourth (although I, for one, would have paid big bucks to see Nicholson play Robin Hood). O'Toole bats 4-for-4.

The film's title does not refer to Alan's favorite year, which presumably happened long before this story began. It is told from the point of view of Benjy Stone, a young television comedy writer played by Mark Linn-Baker.

Written by Dennis Palumbo and Norman Steinberg, the film is very loosely based on an actual incident: Errol Flynn's guest appearance on Sid Caesar's variety show in the 1950s.

Joseph Bologna plays King Kaiser, the film's equivalent of Caesar. Baker's character is reportedly a thinly disguised version of a young Mel Brooks, one of Caesar's writers.

The movie opens with Alan's booking on the program. When the unpredictable actor quickly goes astray, King wants him fired. Benjy, however, speaks up on behalf of his screen idol. He agrees to chaperone Alan to ensure he shows up sober for rehearsals and the live program.

Their adventures together include dinner with Benjy's mother (Lainie Kazan) and uncle (Lou Jacobi), Alan's seduction of another man's date in a nightclub, and his halting attempts to re-establish contact with his long-estranged daughter.

That all leads to the night of the show and Alan's horror when he learns he is expected to perform in front of a live audience without the opportunity for retakes.

Although it runs only ninety-two minutes, the film includes two major subplots—one successful, the other not.

The backstage stuff about live TV in the 1950s is terrific. Bologna is hilarious as the egotistical star who is a genius about comedy but clueless about social graces. As a peace offering to someone he offended, he recommends sending a set of tires.

Bill Macy (not the William H. Macy of *Fargo* fame, but the actor who played Bea Arthur's husband on television's *Maude*) also is very good, as the head writer who constantly blusters against the powers-that-be but quickly caves in when confronted with authority.

> ### *"I'M NOT AN ACTOR. I'M A MOVIE STAR."*
> — PETER O'TOOLE AS ALAN SWANN

Less effective is Benjy's aggressive pursuit of an attractive production assistant, played by Jessica Harper.

Instead of filing sexual harassment charges against her co-worker (admittedly not much of an option in the 1950s), Harper's character surprisingly succumbs to his charms about fifteen minutes after he embarrasses her in front of the crew.

Then, after introducing this romantic element at about the midway point, first-time director Richard Benjamin abruptly drops it for the remainder of the film.

Although a capable actor, Linn-Baker does not quite have the charm to pull off the type of abrasive but lovable wise-guy character that was a specialty of Richard Dreyfuss.

It does not matter, however, since this is clearly O'Toole's film.

The movie's most famous line—Alan's "I'm not an actor. I'm a movie star," uttered when he realizes that he'll have to perform on live TV—would have been good regardless of who spoke it. But the desperate quality O'Toole brought to his delivery made it truly memorable.

An unexpected financial and critical hit, *My Favorite Year* spawned a Broadway musical a decade later, with Tim Curry playing Swann. It quickly flopped.

O'Toole, meanwhile, received the seventh of his record eight unsuccessful Academy Award nominations.

In a normal year, he might have been a strong contender. This time, however, he was caught in the backdraft of a hotly contested three-man Best Actor race involving Dustin Hoffman for *Tootsie,* Paul Newman for *The Verdict,* and the winner, Ben Kingsley for *Gandhi.*

As a consolation prize, King Kaiser might have sent O'Toole a new set of tires. ∎

A PASSAGE TO INDIA

1984

DIRECTOR: DAVID LEAN

PRODUCERS: JOHN BRABOURNE AND RICHARD GOODWIN

SCREENPLAY: DAVID LEAN, FROM BOOKS BY E.M. FORSTER AND SANTHA RAMA RAU

STARRING: JUDY DAVIS AS ADELA QUESTED, VICTOR BANERJEE AS DR. AZIZ AHMED, PEGGY ASHCROFT AS MRS. MOORE

RUNNING TIME: 163 MINUTES

What Alfred Hitchcock was to suspense films, British director David Lean was to what might be termed intelligent epics.

After first building a reputation directing such smaller-scale films as *Brief Encounter,* Lean turned to long movies that covered thought-provoking subjects—the type of productions that later would become the staple of public television's *Masterpiece Theater.*

His films were so visually striking and the stories so engrossing that he was able to hold his audience's attention for approximately three hours.

Lean won Academy Awards for two of those films, *The Bridge on the River Kwai* in 1957 and *Lawrence of Arabia* five years later.

He folowed the latter with a critical and box-office success in *Doctor Zhivago*. But, stung by the negative critical reception for 1970's *Ryan's Daughter*, Lean did not make another movie for 14 years.

His comeback vehicle, *A Passage to India*, was one of his best career efforts.

The topic—the strained relationship between British colonials and India's people in the 1920s—might not have interested many Americans. Those willing to buy into its premise and accept its one hundred and sixty-minute running time, however, found the experience very much worthwhile.

Adapted by Lean from E.M. Forster's novel, the story begins in London.

The proper but sexually repressed young British woman Adela Quested (played by Judy Davis) is about to sail to then-colonial India to reunite with her fiancé, Ronny Heaslop (Nigel Havers), a magistrate in a small Indian province. She is accompanied on the voyage by Ronny's mother, Mrs. Moore (Peggy Ashcroft).

Adela and Mrs. Moore take a strong dislike to the provincial viceroy's dismissive, patronizing attitude toward native Indians. Mrs. Moore, in particular, is subsequently horrified when Ronny displays some of the same characteristics.

A chance encounter results in the women befriending Dr. Aziz Ahmed (Victor Banerjee), an earnest but impoverished Indian physician.

Although the victim of discrimination, Dr. Aziz is touched by Mrs. Moore's gentle nature and agrees to accommodate the women's desire to see "the real India." Too embarrassed to allow them to visit his humble home, he schedules an expedition to the famed Marabar Caves.

Exhausted by the heat and claustrophobic circumstances in the caves, the seventy-something Mrs. Moore stops to rest while Aziz and Adela proceed to explore some of the upper caves.

While Aziz takes a cigarette break, Adela enters one of the caves alone. She emerges moments later bloody and disheveled, eventually accusing Aziz of attempted rape.

Aziz's ensuing trial inflames political passions and ruptures relationships. Refusing to testify against the doctor, Mrs. Moore defies her son and announces her intention to return to England. A post-trial misunderstanding also turns Aziz against another supporter, school superintendent Richard Fielding (James Fox).

> *"LIFE RARELY GIVES US WHAT WE WANT AT THE MOMENT WE CONSIDER APPROPRIATE. ADVENTURES DO OCCUR, BUT NOT PUNCTUALLY."*
> — PEGGY ASHCROFT AS MRS. MOORE

Although the movie is long, the story flags only in a lengthy epilogue—and even that is partially redeemed by an ironic climax.

Sumptuously filmed primarily on location, the film is superbly acted. Honored by rival critics' organizations in both the lead and supporting actress categories, the seventy-seven-year-old Ashcroft won an Academy Award in the latter classification.

The movie received ten other nominations (including Davis for Best Actress), but its only other award went to composer Maurice Jarre.

Life imitated art in the Academy's treatment of Banerjee, who makes his character's transformation from passive geniality to bitterness totally believable. Although the native Indian won the National Board of Review's Best Actor award, he was not even nominated for an Oscar.

Banerjee attended the Academy Award ceremonies intending to accept the Supporting Actress award on behalf of the absent Ashcroft, but was told proxies were not allowed. He was therefore stunned when Angela Lansbury hustled to the podium to collect her friend Ashcroft's statuette.

Lean was a two-time loser on Oscar night for his writing and directing, but the film's critical acclaim restored his reputation and apparently his self-esteem.

Alas, *A Passage to India* was his cinematic swan song. Known for his painstaking attention to detail, he spent seven years planning his next movie (an adaptation of Joseph Conrad's *Nostromo*), but died at age eighty-three before it could be made.

Another project that fell through the cracks was a different take on *Mutiny on the Bounty*. That story eventually was filmed by New Zealand-born director Roger Donaldson as *The Bounty*, with co-stars Mel Gibson and Anthony Hopkins.

While *The Bounty* received respectable reviews, it was widely acknowledged to fall short of greatness.

As many filmmakers learned, there was only one David Lean when it came to making intelligent epics. ■

PRESUMED INNOCENT

1990

DIRECTOR: ALAN J. PAKULA

PRODUCERS: SYDNEY POLLACK AND MARK ROSENBERG

SCREENPLAY: ALAN J. PAKULA AND FRANK PIERSON, BASED ON A NOVEL BY SCOTT TUROW

STARRING: HARRISON FORD AS RUSTY SABICH, BRIAN DENNEHY AS RAYMOND HORGAN, BONNIE BEDELIA AS BARBARA SABICH

RUNNING TIME: 127 MINUTES

A critical and box-office success that featured a top-notch cast and crew, the legal thriller *Presumed Innocent* seemingly had everything necessary to net year-end honors. Everything, perhaps, except good timing.

Adapted from Scott Turow's best-selling novel, the film lacked the gravitas that is normally associated with legitimate Academy Award candidates for Best Picture.

It was so well-acted, however, that I left the theater wondering how many Oscar nominations it would receive.

The correct answer proved to be zero. The film's representatives were excluded not only from the acting categories, but from any Academy Award nominations.

In retrospect, the shutout might have been anticipated. Oscar voters frequently have experienced collective amnesia for movies released before Thanksgiving. *Presumed Innocent* premiered in July.

While not necessarily a masterpiece, the film deserved better.

Harrison Ford stars as Rusty Sabich, a buttoned-down assistant prosecutor whose well-ordered life is spiraling out of control on several fronts.

Since his friend and mentor, prosecuting attorney Raymond Horgan (played by Brian Dennehy), is fighting an uphill battle for re-election, Rusty's job is in jeopardy.

So is his marriage, due to a short-lived affair he had with the seductive, ambitious assistant DA Carolyn Polhemus (Greta Scacchi). Carolyn broke off the relationship, but Rusty continues to be obsessed with her.

Sabich's wife, Barbara (Bonnie Bedelia), an aspiring college professor, remains loving and supportive. But she has not forgotten nor forgiven her husband's infidelity.

Then Carolyn is murdered, and evidence surfaces linking Rusty to the crime.

There are more surprises in store following his arrest—including the once-loyal Raymond (who also had a history with Carolyn) turning on his protege to save his own skin.

Although slowly paced at times and distinctly R-rated in its discussion of sexual matters, this is a smart, absorbing film.

That is not surprising, considering the talent co-producers Sydney Pollack and Mark Rosenberg assigned to the project. Director Alan J. Pakula, screenwriter Frank Pierson (Pakula also assisted with the screenplay), cinematographer Gordon Willis and composer John Williams all ranked among Hollywood's elite.

Pierson and Pakula do a particularly good job of building the tension as the case progresses. The identity of the murderer comes as something of a jolt, even though the clues have been hidden in plain sight.

The acting also is exceptional.

Ford does a solid job of masking his passions behind a constrained exterior. Dennehy is excellent as the duplicitous Raymond, as are Raul Julia as Rusty's flamboyant but savvy defense attorney and Paul Winfield as the trial judge with a large skeleton in his closet.

> ### "I AM A PROSECUTOR. I HAVE SPENT MY LIFE IN THE ASSIGNMENT OF BLAME."
> — HARRISON FORD AS RUSTY SABICH

The biggest victim of the Academy's snub, however, might have been Bedelia.

One of several actresses from the era who seldom received a role worthy of her talent (she is probably best known for playing Bruce Willis' wife in the *Die Hard* series), Bedelia gives added dimensions to what could have been a stock part as the wronged wife. She lets the audience see the love and pain that exist in her emotionally wounded character.

The Best Supporting Actress category was unusually strong that year. Brenda Fricker won for *My Left Foot,* and such renowned performers as Julia Roberts, Dianne Wiest and Anjelica Huston were among the other nominees.

Still, it is all but impossible to watch Bedelia dominate her final scene with Ford without believing she merited some type of Oscar recognition.

The film concludes with Ford's character delivering an unemotional, off-camera epilogue over the backdrop of an empty courtroom. The point seems to be that justice is not always served.

Bedelia and her *Presumed Innocent* colleagues could relate to that sentiment. ∎

QUIZ SHOW

1994

DIRECTOR: ROBERT REDFORD

PRODUCERS: ROBERT REDFORD, MICHAEL JACOBS, JULIAN KRAININ AND MICHAEL NOZIK

SCREENPLAY: PAUL ATTANASIO, FROM THE BOOK *A VOICE FROM THE SIXTIES* BY RICHARD GOODWIN

STARRING: RALPH FIENNES AS CHARLES VAN DOREN, JOHN TURTURRO AS HERBERT STEMPEL, ROB MORROW AS RICHARD GOODWIN

RUNNING TIME: 130 MINUTES

Imagine a category on television's *Jeopardy!* entitled "1990s Movies."

The clue: Robert Redford received his final Academy Award nomination for directing this film about a 1958 scandal.

The answer: What is *Quiz Show?*

Well-acted and directed, Redford's 1994 drama is a very good film. But it could have been better with a more focused final act.

During the mid-1950s, game shows were among the highest-rated programs on television. One of the most popular was *Twenty-One,* a hybrid of the Daily Double portion of *Jeopardy!* and the casino game blackjack.

Contestants answered difficult questions (one example was identifying the man who loaned Paul Revere a horse for his midnight ride) that were assigned varying point totals. As in blackjack, the ultimate goal was to reach exactly twenty-one points.

The public was unaware, however that *Twenty-One* games were rigged (as they were on a few other such programs). Contestants were not only supplied the answers, but much of the on-camera drama also was orchestrated.

As *Quiz Show* opens, nerdish ex-serviceman Herbert Stempel (played by John Turturro) is the reigning *Twenty-One* champion. His abrasive manner, however, is beginning to alienate the audience and the sponsors (legendary director Martin Scorsese has a cameo role as the chief sponsor's representative).

Cold-blooded producer Dan Enright (David Paymer) orders Stempel to intentionally lose to the charismatic challenger Charles Van Doren (Ralph Fiennes), a charming, socially prominent college instructor.

Van Doren initially balks at being a party to a fixed game, but his reservations are overcome by the promise of fame and fortune.

Stempel, who is Jewish, not only is offended at being told to miss a key question he could have answered correctly without assistance but also suspects anti-Semitism figures in Enright's machinations.

Tempted by Enright's empty promise of a future network job, Stempel initially goes along with the plan. But when the job offer falls through and Van Doren becomes a national icon, the bitter ex-serviceman spills the beans to the authorities.

His allegations attract the attention of young congressional aide Richard Goodwin (Rob Morrow). Although finding it difficult to believe that the likable Van Doren (whom he befriends) was complicit, Goodwin launches an investigation to expose the scandal.

Morrow, the quirky doctor on television's *Northern Exposure,* is not quite right for this role. But the remainder of the cast is exceptional.

Turturro, Fiennes and Oscar-nominated Paul Scofield (who played Van Doren's patrician but principled father, poet Mark Van Doren) are excellent. Best of all is veteran character actor Paymer, who is chillingly believable as the producer who might have owned a moral compass at one stage of his life but chucked it into the Hudson River without regret long ago.

Perhaps inevitably, Redford and screenwriter Paul Attanasio were attacked in some quarters for historical discrepancies. Some were pretty minor—a YouTube

> ## "IT'S NOT LIKE WE'RE HARDENED CRIMINALS HERE. WE'RE IN SHOW BUSINESS."
> — HANK AZARIA AS ALBERT FREEDMAN

video clip of the actual Stempel-Van Doren match, for example, reveals Stempel as far less annoying than Turturro's depiction.

But Goodwin's role in the investigation was grossly exaggerated. And the omission of Enright's motivation for initiating the fix (according to several accounts, he believed the questions were so difficult that an honest game would take too long to complete) was inexcusable.

For the most part, the filmmakers do a terrific job of condensing the story into a one hundred and thirty-minute film. The characters are well-developed, and the narrative is absorbing.

A somewhat muted climax, however, leads the audience to wonder about the movie's message.

Is it an indictment of the television industry or the evils of celebrity? Is it a commentary on the gullibility of the viewing public? What was the role of host and co-producer Jack Barry (played in the film by Christopher McDonald) in the fix?

More to the point, what lessons were learned from the episode, and what safeguards, if any, have been employed to prevent a future scandal?

Somehow it is appropriate, however, that a film called *Quiz Show* would contain as many questions as answers. ∎

REAR WINDOW

1954

DIRECTOR: ALFRED HITCHCOCK

PRODUCER: ALFRED HITCHCOCK

SCREENPLAY: JOHN MICHAEL HAYES FROM THE SHORT STORY *IT HAD TO BE MURDER* BY CORNELL WOOLRICH

STARRING: JAMES STEWART AS L.B. "JEFF" JEFFERIES, GRACE KELLY AS LISA FREMONT

RUNNING TIME: 112 MINUTES

Among its many virtues, Alfred Hitchcock's *Rear Window* offers one of the greatest opening scenes in film history. For 140 seconds following the opening credits, the camera scans a New York City apartment while the lead character naps. During that sequence, it is revealed that it is a torrid midsummer day and that the hero is a magazine photographer recovering from a broken leg sustained while he was shooting an auto race.

All of this information is conveyed without a single word. By employing this device, Hitchcock probably saved himself ten minutes of storytelling.

The remainder of the film lives up to that buildup.

The sleeping man is L.B. "Jeff" Jefferies (played by James Stewart), who is in his final week of recuperation and is restless to return to action. His only regular visitors are his fashion-model girlfriend, Lisa Fremont (Grace Kelly), and Stella (Thelma Ritter), a sardonic insurance company nurse.

Out of boredom, Jeff has begun peering out the window at his neighbors in the apartment complex—they include a struggling songwriter, a ballet dancer, a lonely single woman, and a costume jewelry salesman.

Gradually he becomes convinced that the salesman (played by Raymond Burr) has murdered his nagging wife.

The evidence against the salesman is highly circumstantial (and remains so even after some late plot revelations). A police detective friend dismisses Jeff's suspicions out of hand. But Jeff is able to convince the initially skeptical Lisa and Stella, who wind up taking an active part in the investigation. That puts both of them—and the incapacitated Jeff—in peril.

Although many critics rate other films by the legendary director higher, I believe *Rear Window* comes the closest to seamlessly blending all the traditional Hitchcock elements.

It works as a pure thriller, but those who see it as a commentary on voyeurism also have plenty of ammunition. There is a fair amount of humor (most supplied by the scene-stealing Ritter) and a compelling if complicated love story. Despite Lisa's beauty, compassion, fame, and fortune, Jeff keeps trying to avoid commitment by claiming she is "too perfect."

This is a triumph in staging. Hitchcock shoots virtually the entire film from Jeff's apartment, but it never seems claustrophobic.

Immodestly acknowledging he was in a creative mood at the time, Hitch insisted upon adding the girlfriend and nurse (characters who were not in Cornell Woolrich's original short story) to John Michael Hayes' screenplay.

His creativity extends to the casting of small roles. The songwriter, for example, is played by an actual musician, Ross Bagdasarian, the creator of the Chipmunks (thus supplying the elusive missing link between Alfred Hitchcock and Alvin the Chipmunk).

The director slyly settled an old score by making up the thirty-seven-year-old

> "I WONDER IF IT'S ETHICAL TO WATCH A MAN WITH BINOCULARS AND A LONG-FOCUS LENS. DO YOU SUPPOSE IT'S ETHICAL EVEN IF YOU PROVE HE DIDN'T COMMIT A CRIME?"
> — JAMES STEWART AS L.B. JEFFERIES

Burr to resemble white-haired movie magnate David O. Selznick, an old Hitchcock antagonist.

Hitchcock chose the right man for the lead role. With a less likable actor, Jeff easily could have been viewed as a Peeping Tom. Stewart masters a subtly difficult part, reacting to situations and events that the audience can see but the actor could not at the time of the filming.

Kelly's performance is underrated. She's often been described as the consummate Hitchcock heroine, a glamorous blonde whose icy exterior masks hidden passions. But she was a better actress than the vast majority of her imitators. When Jeff tries to discourage her plans for marriage, one can sense Lisa's hurt.

The straitlaced, forty-six-year-old Stewart and the chic Kelly, then in her mid-twenties, might seem an unlikely screen couple. But their love scenes truly crackle, prompting never-answered speculation about an off-screen relationship. The consensus among biographers was that the happily married Stewart, while powerfully attracted to his co-star, resisted the temptation.

As with many Hitchcock films, the plot of *Rear Window* contains some occasional gaps in logic.

Stewart's character would be in far less danger if he bothered to lock his apartment door once in a while, and an insurance company nurse would be unlikely to make evening house calls, as Stella did during the climactic scene.

That doesn't matter in a film this good.

While many of Hitchcock's best movies (such as *Psycho*) were marred by flat endings, *Rear Window* delivers the goods right up to the closing credits. In yet another dialogue-free sequence, all the loose ends are tied up in a final scene that concludes with deliciously ironic humor.

That is *Rear Window*—a great movie from beginning to end. ■

RIO BRAVO

1959

DIRECTOR: HOWARD HAWKS

PRODUCER: HOWARD HAWKS

SCREENPLAY: JULES FURTHMAN AND LEIGH BRACKETT

STARRING: JOHN WAYNE AS SHERIFF JOHN T. CHANCE, DEAN MARTIN AS DUDE

RUNNING TIME: 141 MINUTES

You would never know by watching it, but *Rio Bravo* was designed as something of a message picture.

Producer-director Howard Hawks and star John Wayne disliked two acclaimed Westerns of the 1950s, *High Noon* and the original *3:10 to Yuma*. In both films, lawmen actively sought help from outsiders, which Wayne and Hawks believed painted a false picture of law enforcement in the Old West. They intended to set the record straight with a self-sufficient lawman hero.

While both of the earlier movies are great, *Rio Bravo* is equally entertaining. It overcomes unlikely casting and one of the most improbable scenes in cinematic history to emerge as a classic of the genre.

Wayne stars as John T. Chance, the sheriff of a small Texas town. At the end of a very effective dialogue-free opening sequence, he arrests Joe Burdette (Claude Akins) for killing an unarmed man.

The murder charge predictably does not sit well with Joe's brother Nathan (John Russell), a corrupt rancher who attempts to intimidate the sheriff into releasing his sibling and is willing to resort to stronger tactics if necessary.

Not surprisingly, Wayne's character does not intimidate easily. He also rejects assistance from "well-meaning amateurs," reasoning that they often do more harm than good.

When another killing forces the sheriff to mobilize his forces, the "professionals" he selects include his alcoholic deputy, Dude (Dean Martin); his toothless, limping deputy, Stumpy (Walter Brennan); and a young hired gun, Colorado (Ricky Nelson).

There are those who, when forced to entrust their lives to three men, might choose differently. But, as usually was the case on screen, the Duke knew what he was doing.

A subplot involves John's burgeoning relationship with a professional gambler named Feathers (played by Angie Dickinson). The sheriff originally plans to run Feathers out of town but eventually learns to embrace her— both figuratively and literally.

Dickinson plays a variation of a frequent character in Hawks-directed movies: a talkative woman who takes the initiative in romantic encounters with the male star.

That is the type of role originally played by Lauren Bacall opposite Humphrey Bogart in Hawks' *To Have and Have Not* and *The Big Sleep*, and continued by Joanne Dru in *Red River* and Paula Prentiss in the comedy *Man's Favorite Sport?*

Unlike Bogart and Bacall, Wayne and Dickinson were not in love off-screen. But they generated enough on-screen chemistry to make audiences forget about the twenty-four-year age difference. Cool and confident, Dickinson delivers her best screen performance.

The same can be said for Martin. Casting Dino as a drunk does not sound like much of a stretch, but this is not the lovable tippler from TV celebrity roasts of the 1970s. Here, he is frequently pathetic—particularly in the opening scene, in which

> "SUPPOSING I GOT (MORE HELP). WHAT WOULD I HAVE? SOME WELL-MEANING AMATEURS, MOST OF THEM WORRIED ABOUT THEIR WIVES AND KIDS. BURDETTE HAS 30 OR 40 MEN, ALL PROFESSIONALS. ONLY THING THEY'RE WORRIED ABOUT IS EARNING THEIR PAY."
> — JOHN WAYNE AS JOHN T. CHANCE

he is willing to reach into a spittoon for enough money to buy a drink. Hawks might be the only director who fully tapped Martin's acting potential.

The villains in *Rio Bravo* are curiously bland. Russell, who spent most of his career in television, is so colorless that even fans of the film are hard-pressed to identify the actor who played Wayne's chief adversary.

The heroes are more memorable, with Wayne and Brennan playing roles that fit them like a glove.

This might not be the best Western ever made. But, laced with humor, it might be the most fun to watch. That description even applies to a wildly inappropriate late scene that somehow works almost in spite of itself.

Holed up in the jailhouse during a tense moment waiting for the Burdette gang to attack, Dude and Colorado suddenly break into song by performing a pair of duets.

Needless to say, this scene was not in the original script. Hawks added it after casting Martin and Nelson, believing the audience wanted to hear two of the era's most popular singers do their stuff. Extraneous as it was to the central story, the musical interlude drew few complaints from critics.

Hawks and Wayne liked *Rio Bravo* so much that they essentially remade it twice.

The 1967 Western *El Dorado*—with Robert Mitchum in the Martin role, a young James Caan as a livelier version of Nelson's character, and Christopher George as an unusually principled villain—is almost as good as its obvious inspiration.

But the star and director went to that well once too often with *Rio Lobo* three years later.

Perhaps the latter film might have benefited from a sing-along. ■

THE SET-UP

1949

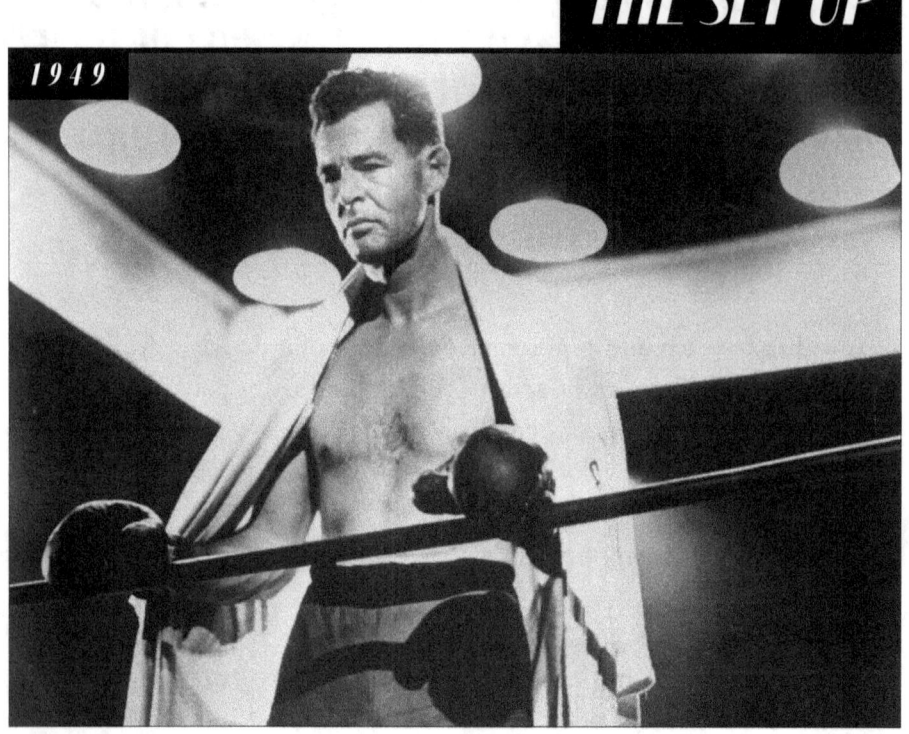

DIRECTOR: **ROBERT WISE**

PRODUCER: **RICHARD GOLDSTONE**

SCREENPLAY: **ART COHN, FROM A NARRATIVE POEM BY JOSEPH MONCURE MARCH**

STARRING: **ROBERT RYAN AS BILL "STOKER" THOMPSON, AUDREY TOTTER AS JULIE THOMPSON**

RUNNING TIME: **72 MINUTES**

Lean and gritty, film noirish in its style, *The Set-Up* has been called one of the greatest boxing movies ever made—even an inspiration for *Raging Bull*.

Not everyone would agree this modestly budgeted production deserves that type of credit. But the 1949 film—based on, of all things, a narrative poem by Joseph Moncure March—is impressively acted. It also provided an admirable launching point for the directorial career of two-time Academy Award winner Robert Wise.

Robert Ryan stars as Bill "Stoker" Thompson, a thirty-five-year-old heavyweight who is reduced to fighting preliminary bouts in which he is invariably the victim of up-and-coming opponents.

He still believes he is one punch away from the big money, but his wife, Julie (Audrey Totter), harbors no such illusions. Loyal but near the end of her emotional rope, she no longer can bring herself to attend her husband's fights. "Maybe you can go on taking the beatings," she tells him. "I cannot."

Stoker's latest stop is the ironically named Paradise City, a tank town in which he is expected to serve as cannon fodder for Tiger Nelson, a promising twenty-three-year-old controlled by icy gangster/gambler Little Boy.

Seeking to protect his investment, Little Boy arranges for the fight to be fixed. Stoker's manager (George Tobias) accepts the money but thinks so little of his fighter's chances that he does not tell Stoker about the arrangement, despite warnings from his trainer (frog-voiced character actor Percy Helton).

That puts Stoker in a classic lose-lose situation by either absorbing another beating or facing Little Boy's postfight wrath.

Wise's decision to film in "real time" was widely hailed by critics, even though the math does not quite work.

The seventy-two-minute film includes sequences at least thirty minutes before and after the program. Most boxing cards, however, are not completed in less than an hour.

In addition, Stoker does not appear battle-scarred or brain-addled enough for someone who has been taking punches for twenty years.

The director's frequent cuts to the crowd, emphasizing the bloodthirsty nature of boxing fans, are overdone. Wise does a good job, though, in replicating the seedy atmosphere of a small fight club.

Ryan received only one Academy Award nomination (for 1947's *Crossfire*), but he spent most of his long career giving Oscar-caliber performances that went unrecognized. This was one of them.

He is tough and delusional, but also tender and frightened when those emotions are appropriate. Ryan's background as a boxing champion at Dartmouth College makes the action sequences exceptionally convincing, although you have to wonder whether Stoker's awkward, lunging style was the actor's own or tailored to fit the character.

Totter gives her best performance as a woman who has accepted her husband's

> *"JUST ONE PUNCH. YOU WERE JUST ONE PUNCH AWAY FROM A TITLE SHOT THEN. DON'T YOU SEE, BILL? YOU'LL ALWAYS BE ONE PUNCH AWAY."*
> — AUDREY TOTTER AS JULIE THOMPSON

career choice but now sees the prospect of permanent injury all too clearly.

Tobias provides an interesting interpretation of the manager—a profession usually depicted in boxing movies as swine. His character is not much better, but more realistic than venal. Stoker does not have a chance, he reasons, so why cut him in on the action?

The solid supporting cast includes Alan Baxter as the soft-spoken but vindictive Little Boy, James Edwards as a young fighter on the way up, and Darryl Hickman as a high school kid making his professional debut.

If the Thompson-Nelson fight unfolds predictably, the bittersweet but realistic final act is far more effective than the melodramatics that generally conclude boxing films.

That might justify the movie's reputation. Even if it was not filmed in real time, *The Set-Up* seems real. ∎

SOUNDER

1972

DIRECTOR: MARTIN RITT

PRODUCER: ROBERT B. RADNITZ

SCREENPLAY: LONNE ELDER III

STARRING: CICELY TYSON AS REBECCA MORGAN, PAUL WINFIELD AS NATHAN LEE MORGAN

RUNNING TIME: 105 MINUTES

Some 50 years after it was made, *Sounder* remains one of the landmark films on the Black experience.

This was the first movie for which a Black screenwriter, Lonne Elder III, received an Academy Award nomination. The film itself was Oscar-nominated. Although it did not feature major stars or contain a great deal of action, it was a substantial box-office hit.

Among films from that era exploring race, it might be the one that holds up best today. That is because it features three exceptional performances and tells a powerful, compelling story without seeming heavy-handed.

Paul Winfield and Cicely Tyson co-star as Nathan Lee and Rebecca Morgan, Depression-era sharecroppers who live on a farm in rural Louisiana.

Frustrated by his inability to put food on the table for his wife and three children through periodic hunting expeditions for raccoons and possums, Nathan resorts to stealing a ham from a neighbor's smokehouse. Arrested for the theft, he is sentenced to a year of hard labor on a prison work gang.

His oldest son, David Lee (played by Kevin Hooks), is thrust into a leadership role at home. But he's also smart and ambitious enough to escape the family's hardscrabble life—possibly by attending an all-Black school he discovers while searching for his father's prison camp.

Although he is off-screen for the middle portion of the film, Winfield has the flashiest role. His character is gregarious and outwardly confident, delighting in his pitching prowess during neighborhood baseball games.

While inwardly insecure about his inability to provide for his family, he treats the family with respect—reflected in the formal handshakes he exchanges with his eldest son.

In a concluding scene, physically broken from his prison-camp experience, he discusses the family's future with David. It is simultaneously heartbreaking and uplifting.

While more subtle, Tyson's performance looks better each time you see the film.

Rebecca knows where the ham came from when Nathan brings it home, but her devotion to her family prevents her from voicing any disapproval.

Particularly in dealing with the white establishment, she has learned to keep her emotions in check. She radiates smoldering resentment in her two scenes with the white store owner who also owns her farm, but never raises her voice.

Tyson and Winfield both received Academy Award nominations. Hooks, who later transitioned from acting to directing, probably should have earned one as well in what is actually the film's central role.

Most of the story is seen through his character's eyes, and he's always convincing as a kid who yearns for a better life but does not want to abandon his parents to get it.

Racism pervades *Sounder,* but Elder and director Martin Ritt wisely let viewers

> **"WHAT DO WE MAKE IT TO, REBECCA? ANOTHER SEASON OF SHARECROPPING FOR OLD MAN PERKINS? WORKING OURSELVES TO DEATH SO HE CAN GET RICHER AND WE CAN'T EVEN EAT WHEN CROPPING TIME IS DONE?"**
> — PAUL WINFIELD AS NATHAN LEE MORGAN

discover it for themselves.

Most fair-minded viewers would agree that the punishment is excessive for Nathan's crime and that the sheriff (James Best, who later played a far more comical lawman on television's *The Dukes of Hazzard*) is hiding his bigotry behind unspecified rules that he claims preclude him from even revealing Nathan's prison-camp whereabouts to his family. Those scenes are handled with a minimum of melodrama.

As with most racially themed films, *Sounder* generated controversy. Some critics contended it reinforced racial stereotypes—an accusation firmly denounced by Tyson, among others.

My only quibble with the film concerns the title, which is the name of the family's dog. The hound accompanies the family on many of its adventures, and its recovery from a gunshot wound symbolizes the Morgans' resiliency. Still, the title might lead some viewers to assume that this is a cuddly animal movie.

Even those people, however, probably will learn something from *Sounder*. ∎

THE STING

1973

DIRECTOR: GEORGE ROY HILL

PRODUCERS: TONY BILL, JULIA PHILLIPS AND MICHAEL PHILLIPS

SCREENPLAY: DAVID S. WARD

STARRING: ROBERT REDFORD AS JOHNNY HOOKER, PAUL NEWMAN AS HENRY GONDORFF

RUNNING TIME: 129 MINUTES

Although it won the 1973 Academy Award for Best Picture, *The Sting* is often condescendingly dismissed by film historians as simply pure entertainment.

I think it is more than that—perhaps the greatest film in a genre Hollywood seldom has mastered.

A few films on con artistry (*House of Games* and *The Grifters* are two examples) have succeeded primarily as character studies. But movies that focus on the con itself invariably have come across as self-consciously clever; deceptive to the audience; or, in some cases, so filled with twists that their very unpredictability became predictable.

Not so with *The Sting*. There are plenty of surprises in David S. Ward's screenplay, but most are based on the audience's assumptions rather than outright deception. Even the eventual sting on the villain depends upon a verbal misunderstanding.

There is no doubt that the film is very entertaining. And, with Robert Redford and Paul Newman playing the leads, there is plenty of star power.

Redford plays Johnny Hooker, a small-time grifter who teams with Luther Coleman (Robert Earl Jones, James Earl's father) to run scams in Depression-era Joliet, Ill. They hit an unexpected jackpot one day when they relieve a courier for New York gangster Doyle Lonnegan (Robert Shaw) of the day's receipts for a numbers game.

Although some of his operatives suggest Doyle simply should forgive and forget, the vengeful mobster orders hits on Johnny and Luther, killing the latter.

Literally outrunning his pursuers, Johnny vows revenge on Doyle but admits he does not know enough about killing to murder him. He settles for a form of financial satisfaction by enlisting the assistance of Henry Gondorff, a specialist in "the big con," in a scheme to bilk the gangster.

Henry (played by Newman) is not exactly living in luxury. On the lam for a federal rap, he is hiding out in a Chicago brothel. He nevertheless agrees to help and is soon assembling a team of grifters for a con so elaborate, it seems highly unlikely it could be put together in the time frame the movie suggests. Suffice it to say, it involves a poker game aboard a train, a horse-racing scam, and dozens of accomplices.

Johnny, meanwhile, is forced to dodge not only Doyle's goons but also a crooked Joliet vice cop and federal agents on Henry's tail.

That sounds like a lot of elements, even for a film that is one hundred and twenty-nine minutes long. But the plot, while tricky, is relatively easy to follow.

Playing a role that Jack Nicholson rejected, Redford received his only Oscar nomination for acting. (He won a directorial Oscar for *Ordinary People*.) It probably is not his best performance, but he does pull off a characterization not normally in his wheelhouse: a good-hearted but none-too-bright grifter attracted to women and gambling.

> **"YOU HAVE TO KEEP THIS CON EVEN AFTER YOU TAKE HIS MONEY. HE CAN'T KNOW YOU TOOK HIM."**
> — PAUL NEWMAN AS HENRY GONDORFF

Newman is fine in a less demanding role. The starring duo is well-supported by a gallery of pros who include Charles Durning, Eileen Brennan, Ray Walston, and Harold Gould.

Acting honors probably belong to Shaw, whose distinctive limp in this film was real (he injured his knee playing handball). As he later demonstrated in the 1974 thriller *The Taking of Pelham 123*, few actors were better at playing icy villains.

His character is hot-tempered and vicious, but also coldly pragmatic. Killing small-time scam artists might seem like an overreaction to some, but the gangster does not want his rivals to get the wrong idea about crossing him.

The film's success, however, is less about acting than about George Roy Hill's jaunty direction, Marvin Hamlisch's memorable score that anachronistically adapted Scott Joplin's turn-of-the-century ragtime music, and Ward's ingenious script. All three won Oscars.

Some critics believe, however, that Ward (only in his twenties at the time) pulled a scam of his own on the Academy. His award for original story and screenplay was questioned by some (including fellow nominee Steve Shagan) who contended it was plagiarized from David S. Maurer's 1940 book *The Big Con*, which also featured a character named Gondorff.

Ward, who was unhappy when Universal Studio executives agreed to an out-of-court settlement on Maurer's eventual lawsuit, asserted that the book was only one of several sources for his story.

But the undistinguished quality of his subsequent work only added fuel to this modest fire. His later screenplays included the disastrous 1983 sequel *The Sting II*.

Ward's story, however, was far from the only problem with the latter film. It also asked audiences to accept Jackie Gleason and singer Mac Davis in the roles originally played by Newman and Redford.

Anyone who bought that casting would be a prime candidate to be victimized by a considerably less complicated con game than the one depicted in *The Sting*. ∎

TALL STORY

1960

DIRECTOR: JOSHUA LOGAN

PRODUCER: JOSHUA LOGAN

SCREENPLAY: JULIUS J. EPSTEIN FROM THE NOVEL *THE HOMECOMING GAME* BY HOWARD NEMEROV AND THE BROADWAY PLAY BY RUSSEL CROUSE AND HOWARD LINDSAY

STARRING: JANE FONDA AS JUNE RYDER, ANTHONY PERKINS AS RAY BLENT

RUNNING TIME: 91 MINUTES

As far as movie debuts go, it is hard to find one stranger than Jane Fonda's.

The Vassar-educated, politically active actress was introduced to big-screen audiences in the romantic comedy *Tall Story,* playing an airheaded, man-hungry college cheerleader named June Ryder.

Stranger yet is that Fonda's co-star might have been even less suited to his role. The object of June's affection—Ray Blent, a supposedly hunky, charismatic All-American basketball player—was portrayed by Anthony Perkins.

The latter casting choice was wrong on several fronts. As he demonstrated in the action scenes of the 1957 baseball biopic *Fear Strikes Out,* Perkins was notoriously unathletic.

In *Tall Story,* director Joshua Logan wisely kept Perkins off the basketball court for the bulk of the film. His character supposedly demonstrates his talent during a climactic game, but only because opposing team members defend him more warily than they would Norman Bates in a shower.

While Perkins was a more versatile actor than his identification with his most famous role in *Psycho* would suggest, his edgy mannerisms made him ill-suited for romantic comedies.

Worse yet, Logan allowed Perkins and Fonda to work out the details of their first big love scene among themselves.

In one of his autobiographies, the director conceded that the scene was slowly paced. "Interminable" would be a more apt description, as the characters engage in discussions of the Japanese method of kissing and the mating habits of elephants (no kidding) before Ray finally makes his move.

Logan wrote that he wanted Warren Beatty (then working in television but still a year away from his star-making role in *Splendor in the Grass*) for Perkins' role, but Warner Brothers executives insisted upon an established leading man.

Had the director been more prescient, he might have noticed an even better choice buried among the film's bit players. Also making his movie debut, in an uncredited role as one of the basketball players, was future Fonda co-star Robert Redford.

By comparison, Fonda comes off pretty well. She likely wasn't comfortable playing a character who embodies stereotypes about female college students, but she at least provides the energy that the role demanded.

June Ryder is introduced when she plows her runaway bicycle into a couple of faculty members at a fictional college. She cheerfully admits that she is attending college only to snare a husband, preferably a member of the school's nationally ranked basketball team.

Her first choice would be Ray, the team's star. Despite his fame, Ray is surprisingly unattached (discussing elephant sex probably has not helped his social life), and June lands him without much difficulty.

Ray is so smitten, in fact, that he is prepared to quit school and marry June, provided he can afford a particularly cozy trailer they can share.

> **"BASKETBALL PLAYERS FLOCK TO CUSTER (COLLEGE), DON'T THEY? THEY'RE USUALLY TALL, AREN'T THEY?"**
> — JANE FONDA AS JUNE RYDER

Such an opportunity arises when he is offered a pile of money from unseen gamblers, if he agrees to fix a big game against a touring Russian national team.

Although it was adapted from a Broadway play, *Tall Story* more closely resembles a 1960s television sitcom. It moves quickly and is easier to take than the plot summary might indicate.

In her memoirs, Fonda describes the making of *Tall Story* as a "Kafkaesque nightmare," writing that she was afflicted with eating disorders and even bouts of sleepwalking. But she devotes surprisingly little space to the film's content.

Perhaps she was secretly relieved that she made her film debut in this piece of fluff instead of the more serious production she had been offered a year earlier. She revealed that she was approached to play the dutiful daughter of a federal agent played by James Stewart in *The FBI Story*.

One of Stewart's biographers contended that Jane was excited about the opportunity but was dissuaded from accepting the role by her father, Henry Fonda. Jane Fonda, however, wrote that she was never interested in the part and went through with the job interview mainly as a courtesy to Stewart—Henry Fonda's best friend.

Imagine Jane Fonda being introduced to big-screen audiences in a movie lionizing an organization that later spent much of the early 1970s investigating her political activities.

Now that would have been a truly weird coming-out party. ∎

THEY WERE EXPENDABLE

1945

DIRECTOR: JOHN FORD

PRODUCER: JOHN FORD

SCREENPLAY: FRANK WEAD AND JAN LUSTIG, BASED ON THE BOOK BY WILLIAM LINDSAY WHITE

STARRING: ROBERT MONTGOMERY AS LT. JOHN BRICKLEY, JOHN WAYNE AS LT. J.G. "RUSTY" RYAN

RUNNING TIME: 135 MINUTES

If ever there were a quality film destined for box-office disaster, it was *They Were Expendable*.

Released just months after World War II ended, this movie depicted one of the war's darkest moments: the Allied evacuation of the Philippines. It contains few action scenes, a muted and truncated love story, and John Wayne in a secondary role.

Not surprisingly, it was neither a critical nor a financial success at the time of its release, although film historian Mark Harris wrote that it at least earned back its $3 million cost at the box office.

More than seventy-five years later, however, it is considered one of the first truly authentic portrayals of World War II combat—a forerunner of sorts to *Saving Private Ryan*. That is a tribute to an intelligent screenplay, well-cast stars, and a legendary director.

Metro-Goldwyn-Mayer studio chief Louis B. Mayer had wanted Oscar-winning director John Ford to make the film as early as 1943, after he obtained the screen rights to a nonfiction best-seller of the same title.

Ford—who was making wartime documentaries as a lieutenant commander in the Navy—had neither the time nor the inclination to accede to Mayer's wishes when he was first approached, but he had second thoughts as his enlistment wound down.

Teaming with screenwriter Frank "Spig" Wead, a World War I Navy pilot, Ford insisted upon going against the grain of most flag-waving war movies. According to Harris, he wanted the film to "offer a message about forgoing maverick impulses or dreams of heroism in favor of the greater good." Indeed, the movie easily could have been called *They Were a Team* or *They Were Professionals*.

Robert Montgomery plays the lead role of Lt. John "Brick" Brickley (the fictional equivalent of Medal of Honor winner John Bulkeley), the commanding officer of a squadron of PT boats stationed in the Philippines on the eve of the war.

To his frustration—and that of his hot-headed executive officer, Rusty Ryan (Wayne)—Brick has been unable to convince the Navy brass of the value of the fast-moving PT boats in combat. Even after the Japanese attack on Pearl Harbor, the squadron is relegated primarily to messenger and transport duty, including the evacuation of Gen. Douglas MacArthur off Corregidor Island.

The unit eventually proves itself in limited combat assignments, but at a price. Brick and Rusty are airlifted back home to oversee the training of replacement PT crews. But they must leave the remainder of their squadron behind to face almost certain capture or death at the hands of the Japanese troops overrunning the Philippines.

In lesser hands, the characters could have been portrayed as tragic or heroic figures. But Ford and Wead have a different agenda.

In their view, the war could be won only by men who put aside their personal glory to follow orders and work as a unit. That is reflected in the film's most famous line: "You and I are professionals. If the manager says sacrifice, we lay down a bunt and let somebody else hit the home runs."

> **"YOU AND I ARE PROFESSIONALS. IF THE MANAGER SAYS SACRIFICE, WE LAY DOWN A BUNT AND LET SOMEBODY ELSE HIT THE HOME RUNS."**
> — CHARLES TROWBRIDGE AS ADM. BLACKWELL TO ROBERT MONTGOMERY AS LT. BRICKLEY

In his admirable book, *Five Came Home,* Harris mistakenly reports that Brick delivered the line to Rusty. It actually was spoken to Brickley by an admiral, played here by white-haired character actor Charles Trowbridge.

While it would be absurd to suggest that Trowbridge upstages the likes of Montgomery and Wayne, his portrayal of a weary, uncompromisingly realistic officer perfectly captures the film's theme.

Assuming a role that studio executives envisioned for Spencer Tracy, Montgomery (who actually skippered PT boats during the war) embodies authority as the calm, purposeful commanding officer. He also directed a few scenes after Ford broke his leg by falling off a scaffold.

Wayne is equally convincing as the fiery second in command. Declaring himself "a one-man band" in an early scene, Rusty is constantly making heroic gestures, only to be reined in by Brick.

In the final scene, he attempts to bolt from the airplane taking him off the island in order to assist his stranded shipmates. He meekly complies with Brick's order, however, when the lieutenant sharply asks, "Who are you working for? Yourself?"

Despite his second billing, Wayne gets more screen time than Montgomery, due in part to a short-lived and nicely understated romance he shares with an Army nurse (well-played by a young Donna Reed). Evidently not flattered by their portrayal, the characters' real-life counterparts sued the filmmakers. Their cases were settled out of court.

Despite the belated recognition Ford and Wead received from critics, neither received an Academy Award nomination for *They Were Expendable.*

But, by setting a standard for authentic war movies, they laid down the sacrifice bunt that allowed later filmmakers to hit home runs with audiences. ∎

THE THIRD MAN

1949

DIRECTOR: CAROL REED

PRODUCERS: CAROL REED, DAVID O. SELZNICK AND ALEXANDER KORDA

SCREENPLAY: GRAHAM GREENE

STARRING: JOSEPH COTTEN AS HOLLY MARTINS, ORSON WELLES AS HARRY LIME

RUNNING TIME: 104 MINUTES

Among its many distinctions, *The Third Man* features what is undoubtedly the most hapless hero for a noncomedy in cinematic history.

As played by Joseph Cotten, American writer Holly Martins is a generally sympathetic character. But, although he has carved out a modest reputation as the author of pulp Western novels, he is all but destitute when he arrives in post–World War II Austria in search of a job.

He drinks too much, uses the wrong name in addressing the head of the British military police force, is loyal to people unworthy of his support, and strikes out spectacularly in attempting to woo the woman he loves.

Those qualities are unusual for a leading man. But *The Third Man* is an unusual film.

As strictly a thriller, it would have been a good movie. What makes it great are its unerring sense of time and place and director Carol Reed's creativity behind the camera.

Holly arrives in war-torn Vienna eager to reunite with longtime friend Harry Lime (played by Orson Welles), an apparently successful entrepreneur. To his shock and dismay, he learns that Harry was supposedly killed when struck by a car.

While investigating the possibility of foul play in the accident, Holly subsequently discovers that (a) Harry made his money through the black-market sale of dangerously diluted penicillin; (b) Harry's actress girlfriend, Anna (Alida Valli), remains devoted to his memory and all but ignores Holly's romantic overtures; and (c) Harry actually still is alive.

Since there is a sense that Orson Welles would not have agreed to play a corpse, the latter revelation shouldn't be as surprising to the audience as it was to Holly. Nevertheless, Reed stages the scene so brilliantly that Harry's first appearance remains an indelible image.

Reed shot this film almost exclusively on location in rubble-strewn Vienna. With Robert Krasker's Oscar-winning cinematography (highlighted by its memorably oblique angles), Anton Karas' zither music, and a group of shadowy character actors, Reed replicates a postwar Europe that is as dark and mysterious as the Vienna sewers where a climactic chase scene takes place.

Offscreen, this production represented a monumental clash of egos involving Reed, Welles, screenwriter Graham Greene, and high-powered filmmakers Alexander Korda and David O. Selznick (the latter two having co-produced the film with Reed).

The notoriously meddlesome Selznick has been criticized in some quarters for many of his suggestions. "His film would have been forgotten in a week," legendary film critic Roger Ebert later contended.

Maybe it is just me, but some of Selznick's ideas did not seem all that bad.

When Reed and Greene differed over the final scene (Greene wanted a happy ending, which the director strongly opposed), Selznick supported Reed's

> "IN ITALY FOR 30 YEARS WITH THE BORGIAS, THEY HAD WARFARE, TERROR, MURDER, AND BLOODSHED. THEY PRODUCED MICHELANGELO, DA VINCI, AND THE RENAISSSANCE. IN SWITZERLAND, THEY HAD BROTHERLY LOVE, AND THEY HAD 500 YEARS OF DEMOCRACY AND PEACE. AND WHAT DID THEY PRODUCE? THE CUCKOO CLOCK."
> — ORSON WELLES AS HARRY LIME

conception of the poignantly downbeat conclusion that became one of the most famous in film history.

Selznick also floated the possibility of Robert Mitchum playing Harry, a prospect that was scuttled when the actor was convicted of marijuana possession.

While Welles' performance as the urbane but sinister Harry was one of his best, Mitchum would have provided a bad-boy charisma that might have made the character even more memorable.

And it was Selznick, who had Cotten under contract, who ultimately was responsible for casting Holly.

This was one instance where the absence of star power actually was beneficial. Cary Grant and James Stewart, who evidently were considered for Holly, would have been far too heroic for the role—and it is hard to envision Valli's character rebuffing Grant the way she did Cotten.

The versatile Cotten, conversely, is totally believable as a socially awkward idealist who is continually disillusioned despite his good intentions.

While *The Third Man* thankfully has yet to be remade for the big screen, it did resurface (at least in title) as a British-American television series in the early 1960s that starred Michael Rennie.

Harry Lime, of all people, was stunningly portrayed as the hero of this version, playing an international private investigator.

As bemused as movie fans might have been over that transformation, the TV producers undoubtedly realized that Holly Martins would have been far too ineffectual for that type of role. ■

TWELVE O'CLOCK HIGH

1949

DIRECTOR: HENRY KING

PRODUCER: DARRYL F. ZANUCK

SCREENPLAY: SY BARTLETT AND BEIRNE LAY JR., FROM THEIR NOVEL (KING MADE UNCREDITED CONTRIBUTIONS)

STARRING: GREGORY PECK AS GEN. FRANK SAVAGE, DEAN JAGGER AS LT. COL. HARVEY STOVALL

RUNNING TIME: 132 MINUTES

Gregory Peck, cinema's archetypal humanistic good guy, would seem an odd choice to play a tough-as-nails general.

When it came to *Twelve O'Clock High,* however, he was an inspired choice.

Peck's stellar performance and the overall authenticity of the screenplay helped make the 1949 drama one of the grittiest and most durable of all World War II films.

With the exception of one late action scene in which actual combat footage is used, the film is confined to a U.S. Army Air Corps base in England.

The story focuses on a unit that specializes in precision daylight bombing of European targets. This particular bomb group has gained a reputation as a hard-luck outfit, due to unusually heavy casualties.

Gen. Frank Savage (played by Peck), the aide to a commanding general, suspects the problem might rest with the unit's popular leader, Col. Keith Davenport (Gary Merrill). Frank believes that Keith, perhaps loyal to a fault, has become overprotective of his flyers and too willing to overlook their shortcomings.

Taking over the unit when Keith is relieved of command, Frank subjects the flyers to an early form of tough love. He enforces rigid discipline and quickly demotes his air executive officer, Lt. Col. Ben Gately (Hugh Marlowe).

Narrowly surviving a mutiny when the flyers demand transfers en masse, Frank begins to get results in the form of improved performance while he rebuilds the men's self-esteem. But the stress of the job begins to get to him, as well.

Screenwriters Sy Bartlett and Beirne Lay Jr., who adapted their own novel for the film, were themselves members of World War II bomb groups and based their story on actual incidents.

Many Air Corps veterans cited *Twelve O'Clock High* as the only Hollywood film that accurately captured their experiences. A scene in which a young flyer tells Frank about his emotions when he returns from missions seems exceptionally true to life.

As he demonstrated when he later played Capt. Ahab in *Moby Dick* and a Nazi in *The Boys from Brazil,* Peck was seldom effective when he strayed far from his standard heroic image. In this case, however, that image helps him sell the character. The audience can sense the humanity lurking beneath Frank's icy exterior.

Director Henry King stages a number of fine scenes—particularly two involving Frank's interaction with Ben.

In the first, described by former *USA Today* critic Mike Clark as one of cinema's greatest chewing-out sequences, Frank accuses Ben of cowardice and dereliction of duty. Frank growls, "I'm just getting started," when the humiliated air exec attempts to terminate the conversation.

Later, after Ben demonstrates his valor by completing a dangerous mission despite a fractured spine, Frank shows his sensitivity by requesting (off-camera) special treatment for Ben while he is recuperating in the hospital.

> **"I WANT YOU TO PAINT THIS NAME ON THE NOSE OF YOUR SHIP: LEPER COLONY. BECAUSE IN IT, YOU'RE GOING TO GET EVERY DEADBEAT IN THE OUTFIT."**
> — GREGORY PECK AS FRANK SAVAGE TO HUGH MARLOWE AS LT. COL. BEN GATELY

Marlowe uses body language to effectively convey his emotions during both scenes.

Although this ranks with Peck's Oscar-winning turn in *To Kill a Mockingbird* as one of his finest performances, he lost the Academy Award for Best Actor that year to Broderick Crawford, for *All the King's Men*.

But Dean Jagger did win the Oscar for Supporting Actor as the unit's ground adjutant, Harvey Stovall.

Jagger did not give the type of flashy scene-stealing performance usually associated with the award. Instead, he subtly created a memorable character who might be the smartest man in the unit. For example, Harvey uses his knowledge of military bureaucracy to delay the pilots' mass transfer requests until Frank can win them over.

The story is seen largely through Harvey's eyes, as the film opens with him visiting the abandoned British airfield following the war, and is told primarily in flashback thereafter.

While that structure makes some narrative sense, it also produces a curiously flat final scene in which Harvey simply rides his bicycle away from the field.

The film also provided a prominent supporting role for Washington state native Robert Arthur, who plays a clerk whom Frank keeps busting and reinstating in rank.

In an interview I conducted with Arthur when he returned to his hometown of Aberdeen some fifty years after the film was completed, the actor surprisingly said he did not enjoy fans reminding him of this role.

"You'd think that was the only movie I ever made," he complained.

But there are worse legacies than to be associated with *Twelve O'Clock High*. ∎

THE VERDICT

1982

DIRECTOR: SIDNEY LUMET

PRODUCERS: DAVID BROWN AND RICHARD ZANUCK

SCREENPLAY: DAVID MAMET, FROM THE NOVEL BY BARRY REED

STARRING: PAUL NEWMAN AS FRANK GALVIN, CHARLOTTE RAMPLING AS LAURA FISCHER, JAMES MASON AS ED CONCANNON

RUNNING TIME: 129 MINUTES

The American Film Institute ranked *The Verdict* the fourth-greatest courtroom drama in cinematic history.

From an entertainment standpoint, it deserves that distinction. In terms of authenticity, not so much.

The film's misrepresentation of legal procedures caused attorneys at the time to howl—both in protest and laughter. Yet the story is so well told and impeccably acted that the deviations from accuracy almost do not matter.

Paul Newman stars as Frank Galvin, a once-promising Boston attorney on the skids. Framed in a jury-tampering case, fired, and divorced by the daughter of his legal firm's managing partner, he has descended into a barely functional life as an alcoholic ambulance-chaser.

His retired former law partner, played by Jack Warden, tries to throw some business his way in the form of an apparent slam-dunk malpractice case in which a young woman was left comatose.

Everyone seemingly wants to settle matters out of court. The Catholic archdiocese that operates the hospital in question does not want unfavorable publicity. Frank badly needs the money from a settlement, as do his clients (the woman's sister and brother-in-law), who want to start a new life in Arizona.

Since this film is not called *The Settlement,* the audience senses that Frank will head in a different direction.

His dormant idealism rekindled by a visit to the nursing home where the victim is housed, he unilaterally rejects the archdiocese's offer and decides to try the case. "'Cause if I take the money, I've lost. I'll just be a rich ambulance-chaser," he explains.

That is all well and good, but his decision upsets his clients and antagonizes the crooked judge assigned to hear the case.

It also puts him in conflict with the well-heeled law firm headed by the smooth but unscrupulous Ed Concannon (James Mason) that is representing the doctors and the church. Ed begins by buying off Frank's chief witness—and he's just warming up.

In *Law for Writers,* Stephen Terrell contends that this movie is "hideous" from a legal sense. By failing to inform his clients of the settlement offer, Frank breaks the rules of professional accountability and almost certainly would be subject to sanctions.

Frank's introduction of a last-minute witness without notifying the defense likely would be thrown out on appeal. His closing summation is essentially philosophical mumbo-jumbo that might not have swayed a jury in a jaywalking trial.

Perhaps more to the point, legal scholars have suggested that a series of unfavorable rulings issued by the judge left Frank literally without a case.

But as he demonstrated five years later with his historically deficient but entertaining screenplay for *The Untouchables,* screenwriter David Mamet has such a knack for characterization and storytelling that the audience will forgive

> **"I CAME HERE TO TAKE YOUR MONEY ... I CAN'T DO IT; I CAN'T TAKE IT. 'CAUSE IF I TAKE IT, I'M LOST. I'LL JUST BE A RICH AMBULANCE-CHASER."**
> — PAUL NEWMAN AS FRANK GALVIN

transgressions in other areas.

Some twenty-five years after he began his filmmaking career with another acclaimed courtroom drama, *12 Angry Men,* Sidney Lumet directs with his customary precision and eye for detail.

The exceptional supporting cast includes Charlotte Rampling as Frank's mysterious girlfriend, Milo O'Shea as the judge on the take, the always-underrated Warden and the Oscar-nominated Mason. Lindsay Crouse is stunning in the small role of Frank's surprise witness, a former nurse who reluctantly revisits her involvement in the tragedy.

In his 1994 book, *If the Other Guy Isn't Jack Nicholson, I've Got the Part,* Ron Base reported that Robert Redford initially had agreed to play the lead. But, protective of his image as an actor, Redford did not want to play Frank as a drunk or a loser. "When he realized he'd have to let the warts show, let it all hang out, then he backed off," co-producer Richard Zanuck later recounted.

But Newman had no such qualms. Even when sober, Frank is hardly a paragon of virtue. Playing pinball in a bar, he almost misses an important pretrial conference. Later, he assaults a woman and commits a federal offense by tampering with the mail.

Newman always lets the audience see the desperation lurking beneath his outward bravado. He lost the Best Actor Academy Award to Ben Kingsley (for *Gandhi*), but his Oscar for *The Color of Money* four years later might have been a makeup call of sorts.

In the first draft of the screenplay, Mamet reportedly had the very bad idea of ending *The Verdict* before the verdict actually was announced.

Saner heads prevailed, and the film closes with a much-debated scene in which Frank sits deep in thought while refusing to answer a ringing telephone.

What he's thinking is never made clear. My guess is that he is wondering how much simpler his life would have been had he taken the settlement offer. ■

WRITTEN ON THE WIND

1956

DIRECTOR: DOUGLAS SIRK

PRODUCER: ALBERT ZUGSMITH

SCREENPLAY: GEORGE ZUCKERMAN, BASED ON THE BOOK BY ROBERT WILDER

STARRING: ROCK HUDSON AS MITCH WAYNE, LAUREN BACALL AS LUCY HADLEY, ROBERT STACK AS KYLE HADLEY

RUNNING TIME: 99 MINUTES

Even for those who do not care for melodramas, the opening scene in *Written on the Wind* is a grabber.

A sports car speeds erratically down a lonely, windswept Texas road. As if to answer any questions about the driver's sobriety, he is shown openly swigging from a whiskey bottle—which he hurls theatrically against the side of a mansion upon reaching his destination.

Waiting nervously inside are the driver's wife, sister, and best friend, all of whom have reasons to dread his arrival. Moments later, a shot rings out, and someone (the body is partially obscured by shrubbery) staggers outside, fatally wounded.

All of this action is played out over the opening credits, accompanied by the Four Aces' rendition of the title tune. Songwriter Sammy Cahn evidently was not provided with a copy of the script, since his lyrics bear scant resemblance to the plot.

Kind of makes you want to see the rest of the movie, right?

Most of the remainder of the film is told in flashback. The driver is Kyle Hadley (played by Robert Stack), an alcoholic playboy who is the presumed heir to his father's oil company. On a trip to New York, he becomes smitten with chic executive secretary Lucy Moore (Lauren Bacall).

Kyle is soon flying Lucy to a weekend in Florida. His best friend is a geologist named Mitch Wayne — played by Rock (pun apparently not intended) Hudson — who rather awkwardly tags along. Despite some misgivings, Lucy ultimately accepts Kyle's marriage proposal.

As the opening scene suggests, this is not a relationship destined to end well. Kyle attempts to settle down, but his frustration over his apparent inability to father a child and Mitch's growing interest in Lucy drive him back to the bottle.

Meanwhile, Kyle's promiscuous sister Marylee (Dorothy Malone), who has carried an unrequited torch for Mitch since childhood, is more than willing to fuel her brother's jealousy by spreading false rumors about Mitch and Lucy.

All of this is neatly packaged into a ninety-nine-minute film, which also contains a bar fight, an incident of domestic violence, a couple of accidental deaths, a murder trial, and a hilariously lurid scene in which Marylee seduces a gas-station attendant.

One scene that probably would not make it into a remake: Despondent over the apparently hopeless nature of his attraction to Lucy, Mitch tells his father he is considering seeking employment in Iran.

This film was directed by Douglas Sirk, a German emigre who worked in a variety of genres but is best known for the series of melodramas (many starring Hudson) that he made during the 1950s.

Movie historian Charles Matthews wrote that Sirk's "undeniable if dubious talent was [that] he took melodramatic chestnuts...seriously enough to make them entertaining."

> **"WE'RE TROUBLESHOOTERS. WHEREVER THEY WANT TROUBLE, THEY SEND FOR US."**
> — ROBERT STACK AS KYLE HADLEY

That is true enough, but Sirk was also a good storyteller with a gift for visualizing emotional anguish. Even when his plots are over the top, it is hard to turn away from them.

Malone won an Academy Award for Supporting Actress, and many expected Stack to follow suit in the Supporting Actor category. (The upset winner there was Anthony Quinn, for his small but vital role as artist Paul Gauguin in the Vincent Van Gogh biopic *Lust for Life*.)

Some critics contend that the supporting players stole the film from the nominal leads. I cannot bring myself to agree.

Malone gives a florid performance that represents a master class in scenery-chewing.

Stack, who specialized in stolid but macho authority figures (an image he wickedly parodied in 1980's *Airplane!*), plays a man here who does not embody either quality. He works like the devil to portray a charismatic but weak character that would have been tailor-made for someone like Montgomery Clift, but he's never quite convincing in the role.

Bacall was the most accomplished performer of the featured quartet, but she suffers from the screenplay's inability to develop her character. Does the presumably intelligent Lucy marry Kyle out of love, pity, or financial security? Even at the end, the audience does not know.

Hudson's limitations as an actor have been well-documented, but he often was convincing working within those limitations. His lovestruck but principled character is the film's most believable.

Considering the effectiveness of the flashback sequences, the climax to *Written on the Wind* is something of a disappointment. The ultimate murder trial is given short shrift, and the accompanying revelations produce few surprises.

The film ends with another car leaving the Texas mansion. Its destination is never revealed, but it probably is not Iran. ■

ZERO HOUR! & AIRPLANE!
1957 / 1980

ZERO HOUR!

DIRECTOR: HALL BARTLETT

PRODUCERS: HALL BARTLETT AND JOHN CHAMPION

SCREENPLAY: HALL BARTLETT, JOHN CHAMPION, AND ARTHUR HAILEY, FROM HAILEY'S TELEPLAY *FLIGHT TO DANGER*

STARRING: DANA ANDREWS AS TED STRYKER, LINDA DARNELL AS ELLEN STRYKER, STERLING HAYDEN AS MARTIN TRELEAVEN

RUNNING TIME: 81 MINUTES

DIRECTORS: JIM ABRAHAMS, DAVID ZUCKER, AND JERRY ZUCKER

PRODUCER: JON DAVISON

SCREENPLAY: JIM ABRAHAMS, DAVID ZUCKER, AND JERRY ZUCKER

STARRING: ROBERT HAYS AS TED STRIKER, JULIE HAGERTY AS ELAINE DICKINSON, LESLIE NIELSEN AS DR. RUMACK

RUNNING TIME: 86 MINUTES

To a certain audience, *Zero Hour!* strangely might be regarded as one of the funniest movies ever made.

Strange, in that the 1957 film was intended to be a deadly serious thriller.

Dana Andrews stars as Ted Stryker, a former Canadian fighter pilot whose adjustment to civilian life is complicated by his experiences in World War II. Haunted by an ill-fated bomber raid in which his decision-making resulted in numerous fatalities, he has experienced difficulty keeping jobs in the decade following the war. His wife (played by Linda Darnell) is preparing to leave him and take their young son with her.

Although terrified of flying since the war, the distraught Stryker boards the flight on which his family is traveling from Winnipeg to Vancouver.

When both pilots and many of the passengers are stricken with food poisoning, he is recruited to land the plane in difficult weather conditions. Complicating the process is the mutual hostility between Stryker and the hard-as-nails former wartime colleague (Sterling Hayden) that the airline assigns to talk him down.

If that plot sounds familiar to younger audiences, it is because it was recycled almost intact for the enormously popular and outrageously funny 1980 parody, *Airplane!*

In the latter movie, Robert Hays plays the Andrews role, Julie Hagerty has Darnell's, Robert Stack and Lloyd Bridges take portions of Hayden's character, and Leslie Nielsen plays a doctor on board (portrayed by virtual lookalike Geoffrey Toone in the earlier film).

There is even an athlete-in-the-cockpit casting similarity. Basketball great Kareem Abdul-Jabbar spoofed his own image as a co-pilot in *Airplane!* Football Hall of Famer Elroy "Crazylegs" Hirsch was one of the stricken pilots in *Zero Hour!* Winding up a brief, unsuccessful acting career, Hirsch was about as animated as the inflatable automatic pilot Otto in the later film.

> "THE LIFE OF EVERYONE ON BOARD DEPENDS ON JUST ONE THING: FINDING SOMEONE WHO CAN NOT ONLY FLY THIS PLANE BUT DIDN'T HAVE FISH FOR DINNER."
> — GEOFFREY TOONE AS DR. BAIRD

Writer-directors Jim Abrahams and Jerry and David Zucker borrowed plot elements from several classic films, most notably the 1970 blockbuster *Airport*. But *Zero Hour!* provides the basic structure, to the point where Abrahams and the Zuckers purchased the rights to that film so they could plagiarize it with impunity. Even the lead character's name is the same (although spelled differently) in both films.

The most famous exchange from *Airplane!* ("Surely, you can't be serious." "I am serious, and don't call me Shirley.") has no counterpart in *Zero Hour!*—but other dialogue from the earlier film is lifted verbatim. The doctor in *Zero Hour!* actually utters the line, "The life of everyone on board depends on just one thing: Finding someone who can not only fly this plane but didn't have fish for dinner."

More often than not, Abrahams and the Zuckers put their own zany spin on the original material.

The Hayden character, for example, muses that he picked the wrong week to quit smoking. Bridges not only repeats that line, but recycles it in several forms, concluding by saying he picked the wrong week to quit sniffing glue.

The *Airplane!* filmmaking trio made two decisions that contributed to their film's success. Instead of hiring comedians who might have pushed the gags too

> ## "SURELY, YOU CAN'T BE SERIOUS."
> — ROBERT HAYS AS TED STRIKER

hard, they filled the supporting cast with such veteran deadpan actors as Nielsen, Stack, Bridges, and Peter Graves, who played their roles relatively straight. Hays also nicely underplays the lead role.

A serious dramatic actor previously, Nielsen reinvented himself by appearing in broad comedies for the remainder of his career. Stack, who is a riot, might have done his best work here in either comedy or drama.

The filmmakers also found the perfect inspiration for a comedic remake. Judged on its own merits, *Zero Hour!* was not a bad entry in the disaster-in-the-sky genre. But its self-important tone and melodramatic dialogue made it a ripe target for satire.

Watching *Airplane!* more than once, the audience might be struck by the amount of humor that does not work. But the gags come so fast and furious that before viewers can negatively respond to a bad joke, a better one arrives.

The surprise box-office success of this film inspired a raft of imitations—most of them sophomoric. But the market for this genre (if broad parodies can be called a genre) dried up quickly. Abrahams and the Zuckers split up.

In any event, the final installment of Nielsen's *Naked Gun* trilogy (which was released in 1994) was the last truly successful film of its kind. As most of the imitators sadly discovered, pulling off a broad comedic parody was much more difficult than it appeared.

Fans nostalgic for that type of film, however, always can check out *Zero Hour!* If they do not find it unintentionally hilarious, they might have picked the wrong week to quit sniffing glue. ■

> ## "I AM SERIOUS, AND DON'T CALL ME SHIRLEY."
> — LESLIE NIELSEN AS DR. RUMACK

INDEX

Numbers
12 Angry Men, 144
1776, 77
3:10 to Yuma, 1–3, 118

A
A Beautiful Mind, 12
A Date With Judy, ii, 46, 48
A Few Good Men, 33
A League of Their Own, 82
A Passage to India, 106–108
A Streetcar Named Desire, 24
Abbott, Elliot, 82
Abrahams, Jim, 148, 150
Absence of Malice, 4–6
Academy Awards, ii, 6, 8, 15, 27, 53, 107
The Accidental Tourist, 17
Adams, Julia, 23
Adams, Lee, 28
Adams, Sam, 77
The Adventures of Robin Hood, 41–42
The African Queen, 24
Aherne, Brian, 75
Airplane!, 147–151
Akins, Claude, 119
Albertson, Jack, 96
All About Eve, 90
All Quiet on the Western Front, 76
All the King's Men, 35, 141
All the President's Men, 4–5
Allen, Woody, ii
Altman, Aaron, 25–27
Altman, Robert, ii
Ambush at Blanco Canyon, 19
The American Film Institute, i, 142
American Revolution, 77
Anatomy of a Murder, 7–9
Andrews, Dana, 148–149
Andrews, Julie, 102
Ann-Margret, 28–30
Annie Get Your Gun, 30
Anthelme, Paul, 73
Apollo 13, ii, 10–12
Archibald, William, 73, 75
Arden, Eve, 8
Armstrong, Neil, 11
Arthur, Bea, 104
Arthur, Robert, 141
Ashcroft, Peggy, 106–108
Asinof, Eliot, 61, 63
Attanasio, Paul, 112–113
Attenborough, Richard, 71
Azaria, Hank, 114

B
Bacall, Lauren, 119, 145–146
Backus, Jim, 24
Bacon, Kevin, 10–11
Bad Day at Black Rock, 13–14, 72
Bad Time at Honda, 13–14
Bagdasarian, Ross, 116
Baker, Carroll, 19

Baldwin, Alec, 92
Bale, Christian, 2
Banerjee, Victor, 106–107
Bartlett, Hall, 148
Bartlett, Sy, 19, 139–140
Base, Ron, 144
Based on a True Story, 68
Bates, Norman, 103, 131
Batman, 54
Baxter, Alan, 123
Baxter, Anne, 73–74, 90
The Beatles, 102
Beatty, Warren, 131
Becher, Irving, 28
Beckett, Scotty, 47
Bedelia, Bonnie, 109–110
Beery, Wallace, 46
Beloin, Edmund, 85
Ben-Hur, 20–21
Benedek, Barbara, 16
Benjamin, Richard, 103, 105
Bennett, Tony, 68
Benson, Helen, 52, 54
Berenger, Tom, 17
Bergman, Ingrid, 74
Bergman, Jules, 12
Bernstein, Elmer, 72
Best, James, 126
The Best Years of Our Lives, 21
Beymer, Richard, 78
Bickford, Charles, 20
Biegler, Paul, 7–9
The Big Chill, 16–18
The Big Con, 129
The Big Country, ii, 19–21

The Big Sleep, 119
Bill, Tony, 127
Birdie, Conrad, 29
Bjork, Anita, 74
Blackburn, Tom, 76–77
Blaine, Rick, 103
Blankfort, Michael, 31
Blaustein, Julian, 52–53
Bodine, Kyle, 37–39
Body Heat, 17, 37–39
Bogart, Humphrey, 24, 31–33, 55, 57, 119
Bogdanovich, Peter, 74
Bologna, Joseph, 104
The Bonfire of the Vanities, 84
Bonnie and Clyde, 29
Borgnine, Ernest, 14
The Bounty, 108
Boyle, Peter, 34–35
The Boys from Brazil, 140
Brabourne, John, 106
Bracco, Lorraine, 68, 91
Brando, Marlon, 23, 98–99
Braugher, Andre, 66
Brennan, Eileen, 129
Brennan, Walter, 15, 119
The Brick Foxhole, 43
Brickhill, Paul, 70
The Bridge on the River Kwai, 107
Bridges, Jeff, 93
Brief Encounter, 106
Bright Victory, ii, 22–24
Brimley, Wilford, 6
Broadcast News, i–ii, 25–27, 168
Broderick, Matthew, 64–66

Bronson, Charles, 71
Brooks, Albert, 25–27
Brooks, James, 26–27
Brooks, Mel, 104
Brooks, Richard, 43
Brown, David, 142
Brown, Jerry, 35
Brown, Pat, 35
Broyles, William, 10
Bruns, George, 77
Bryant, Anita, 102
Buckner, Robert, 22
Bulkeley, John, 134
Burchard, Peter, 64
Burnett, W.R., 70, 72
Burns, Mark, 91
Burr, Raymond, 18, 116
Bye Bye Birdie, 28–30

C

Caan, James, 120
Cabot, Sebastian, 77
Cage, Nicolas, 79
Cahn, Sammy, 146
The Caine Mutiny, ii, 8, 24, 31–33, 58, 168
The Caine Mutiny Court-Martial, 32
Candaele, Kelly, 82
The Candidate, 34–36
Carlson, Roy, 37
Carlton, Nick, 16
Cartwright, Ben, 20
Caruso, David, 79
Casablanca, i, 103
Caspary, Vera, 88

Cat on a Hot Tin Roof, 20
Champion, Gower, 28
Champion, John, 148
Chance, John T., 118–120
Cher, 27
Chicago White Sox, 61–63
China Moon, ii, 37–39
Chinatown, i
Cincinnati Reds, 62–63
Citizen Kane, i
Civil War, 64, 66
Clark, Fred, 86
Clark, Mike, 140
Clavell, James, 70, 72
Clift, Montgomery, 73–74, 147
Close, Glenn, 16–18
Coblenz, Walter, 34
Coburn, James, 71
Cohn, Art, 121
Cohn, Harry, 33
The Color of Money, 144
Comiskey, Charles, 62
I Confess, ii, 73–75
Cooper, Dorothy, 46
Cooper, Harold, 16
Cooper, Sarah, 16–18
Cosmopolitan, 89–90
Costner, Kevin, 17
Cotten, Joseph, 136
The Court Jester, 40–42
The Courteous Hours, 57
Crain, Jeanne, 88–90
Crawford, Broderick, 141
Crenna, Richard, 38
Crimson Tide, 33

Cronkite, Walter, 12
Crosby, Bing, 41, 85, 87
Crossfire, 43–45, 122
Crouse, Lindsay, 144
Crouse, Russel, 130
Crowe, Russell, 2
Cugat, Xavier, 46
Curry, Tim, 105
Cusack, Joan, 26, 92
Cusack, John, 61–62

D
DaCosta, Morton, 100
The Daily World, i, iii, 168
Dana, Leora, 3
Dance, Charles, 38
Dark Victory, 22
Darnell, Linda, 88–89, 148–149
Dave, 49–51
Daves, Delmer, 1–2
Davies, Valentine, 94
Davis, Bette, 22
Davis, Geena, 82–83
Davis, Judy, 106–107
Davis, Mac, 129
Davison, Jon, 148
The Day the Earth Stood Still, 52–54
De Niro, Robert, 67–68
The Defiant Ones, 33
Del Toro, Benicio, 38
Demme, Jonathan, 91
Dennehy, Brian, 84, 109–110
Depp, Johnny, 18
Desperate Hours (1990), 55
The Desperate Hours, ii, 55–57

The Devil's Disciple, 77
Dickinson, Angie, 119
Dillon, Melinda, 5
Disney, Walt, 76–77
Dmytryk, Edward, 31–32, 43, 45
Doctor Zhivago, 107
Donaldson, Roger, 108
Donlevy, Brian, 80
Donner, Lauren Shuler, 49
Doren, Mark Van, 113
On the Double, 42
Douglas, Helen Gahagan, 36
Douglas, Kirk, 89
Douglas, Paul, 89–90
Dow, Peggy, 22–23
Dratler, Jay, 55
Dreyfuss, Richard, 105
Drive a Crooked Road, ii, 58–60
Dru, Joanne, 119
Drums Along the Mohawk, 76
Dugan, Jimmy, 82–84
The Dukes of Hazzard, 126
Dunaway, Faye, 6
Dunnock, Mildred, 81
Durning, Charles, 129

E
Ebert, Roger, i, 1, 65, 137, 167
The Ed Sullivan Show, 29
Edwards, Blake, 58–59
Edwards, James, 23, 123
Eight Men Out, ii, 61–63
El Dorado, 120
Elder III, Lonne, 124
Elinson, Irving, 85

The Enemy Below, 14
Evans, Ray, 87

F

The Fabulous Baker Boys, 93
Fargo, ii, 104
Farr, Felicia, 2
The FBI Story, 132
Fear Strikes Out, 131
Ferrer, José, 31, 33
Field of Dreams, 69
Field, Sally, 4–5, 97, 99
Fields, Freddie, 64
Fiennes, Ralph, 112–113
A Fish Called Wanda, 93
The Fisher King, 93
Five Came Home, 135
Flynn, Errol, 41, 103–104
Fonda, Henry, 32, 73, 132
Fonda, Jane, 6, 130, 132
Forbes, Esther, 76–77
Ford, Glenn, 1–3
Ford, Harrison, 109–111
Ford, John, 60, 76, 133–134
Foreign Correspondent, 96
Forster, E.M., 106–107
Foster, Dianne, 58–60
Fox, James, 107
Foxx, Jimmie, 84
Francis, Freddie, 65
Frank, Harriet Jr., 97–98
Frank, Melvin, 40–41
Frawley, William, 96
Freeman, Morgan, 64–65
Fricker, Brenda, 111

Full Metal Jacket, 92
Furthman, Jules, 118

G

Galloway, Don, 18
Gandhi, 105, 144
Gandil, Chick, 62
Ganz, Lowell, 82
Garland, Judy, 58–59
Garner, James, 70–71, 97, 99
Gauguin, Paul, 147
Gautier, Dick, 30
Gazzara, Ben, 8
Geer, Will, 24
Gentleman's Agreement, 45
George, Christopher, 120
Gibson, Mel, 77, 108
Gingold, Hermione, 102
Gleason, Jackie, 129
Glory, 64–66
The Godfather, i
Goldblum, Jeff, 17
Goldstone, Richard, 121
Goldwyn, Samuel, 70
Gondorff, Henry, 127–129
Gone With the Wind, ii
The Gong Show, 38
GoodFellas, i, 67–69, 91
Goodwin, Richard, 106, 112–113
Gould, Harold, 129
Grahame, Gloria, 44
Grand Canyon, 17
Grant, Cary, 101, 138
Graves, Peter, 151
Gray, Billy, 54

Gray, Coleen, 79-81
Grazer, Brian, 10
The Great Escape, 70–72
The Great Movies series, i–ii
Greene, Graham, 136–137
Greenhut, Robert, 82
Griffin, Glenn, 55–57
The Grifters, 127
Griswold, Sir, 41
Grodin, Charles, 51
Gross Anatomy, 92
Grunick, Tom, 25–26
Gruskoff, Michael, 103
Guess Who's Coming to Dinner, 33
Gunfight at the OK Corral, 72
Gwendolyn, Princess, 41
Gwenn, Edmund, 81, 94–95

H

Haas, Dolly, 75
Hagerty, Julie, 148–149
Hailey, Arthur, 148
Haim, Corey, 98
Hall, Porter, 96
Hamilton, Donald, 19
Hamlisch, Marvin, 129
Haney, Lynn, 21
Hanks, Tom, 10–12, 82–84, 93
Hans Christian Andersen, 41
Hargrove, Marion, 100
Harper, Jessica, 105
Harris, Ed, 11, 37–39
Harris, Mark, 133
Hartmann, Edmund, 85
Harvey, Walter, 83

Hasse, O.E., 74–75
Hathaway, Henry, 79
To Have and Have Not, 119
Havers, Nigel, 107
Hawks, Howard, 1, 118
Hayden, Sterling, 148–149
Hayes, John Michael, 115–116
Hayes, Joseph, 55
Hays, Robert, 148–149, 151
Hecht, Ben, 79
Heflin, Van, 1–2
Heilweil, David, 1
Helton, Percy, 122
Hepburn, Audrey, 102
Herrmann, Bernard, 53
Heston, Charlton, 19–21
Hickman, Darryl, 123
High Noon, 1, 118
Hill, George Roy, 127, 129
Hill, Harold, 100–102
Hill, Henry, 67, 69
Hirsch, Elroy "Crazylegs," 149
Hirt, Al, 102
Hitchcock, Alfred, 73, 96, 106, 115–116
Hoffman, Dustin, 105
Hollingsway, Lora Mae, 88–90
Hollingsway, Porter, 88–90
Holm, Celeste, 90
Home of the Brave, 24
Hondo, 14
Hooks, Kevin, 125
Hope, Bob, 42, 85, 87
Hopkins, Anthony, 55, 108
Horner, James, 65

House of Games, 127
Howard, Ron, 10–11, 102
Hud, 98
Hudson, Rock, 24, 145–147
Hunter, Holly, 25, 27, 168
Hurt, William, 16–17, 25, 38
Huston, Anjelica, 111

I

If the Other Guy Isn't Jack Nicholson, 144
Ireland, Jill, 71
Ives, Burl, 20

J

Jabbar, Kareem Abdul, 149
Jackson, "Shoeless" Joe, 62, 69
Jacobs, Michael, 112
Jagger, Dean, 14, 139, 141
Jarmon, Crocker, 34
Jarre, Kevin, 64
Jarre, Maurice, 108
Jewison, Norman, 27
Johnny Tremain, 76–78
Johns, Glynis, 40–41
Johnson, Van, 31–32
Jones, Murphy, 97–99
Jones, Robert Earl, 128
Jones, Shirley, 100-102
Joplin, Scott, 129
Judgment at Nuremberg, 33
Julia, Raul, 110

K

Kansas City Confidential, 81

Karas, Anton, 137
Kasdan, Lawrence, 16–17
Kaufman, Millard, 13, 15
Kaye, Danny, 40, 42, 101
Kaye, Sylvia Fine, 41
Kazan, Lainie, 104
Kelly, Gene, 101
Kelly, Grace, 115–116
Kelly, Jack, 59
Kelly, Paul, 44
Kelton, Pert, 102
Kendrick, Baynard, 22–23
Kennedy, Arthur, 22–24, 56
Kerwin, Brian, 98
King, Henry, 139–140
Kingsley, Ben, 50, 105, 144
Kingsley, Dorothy, 46
Kirstein, Lincoln, 64
Kiss of Death, 79–81
Kiss Me Kate, 30
Klempner, John, 88
Kline, Kevin, 16–17, 49–51, 93
Kluger, Jeffrey, 10
Kobish, Simon, 56
Kohlmar, Fred, 28, 79
Korda, Alexander, 136–137
Krainin, Julian, 112
Kramer, Stanley, 23, 31–32
Kranz, Gene, 11
Krasker, Robert, 137

L

Ladd, Alan, 15
Laine, Frankie, 3
Lancaster, Burt, 59, 101

Lanfield, Sidney, 85, 87
Langella, Frank, 50
Lansbury, Angela, 41, 108, 168
Lapham, Priscilla, 76–77
Lardner, Ring, 62
Larner, Jeremy, 34–35
Law for Writers, 143
Lawrence of Arabia, 107
Lay, Beirne Jr., 139
Lean, David, 106, 108
Lederer, Charles, 79
Leigh, Janet, 28–29
The Lemon Drop Kid, ii, 85–87
Lerner, Michael, 62
Les Miserables, 54
Leslie, Aleen, 46
Letter to Three Wives, 88–90
Levene, Sam, 44
Lindsay, Howard, 130
Lindsay, John, 35
Linn-Baker, Mark, 103–104
Liotta, Ray, 67, 69
Lipsky, Eleazar, 79
Livingston, Jay, 87
Lloyd, Christopher, 62
Lockhart, Gene, 96
Logan, Joshua, 130–131
Lovitz, Jon, 83
Lucas, Marvin, 34–35
Luedtke, Kurt, 4–5
Lumet, Sidney, 142, 144
Lust for Life, 147
Lustig, Jan, 133
Lynde, Paul, 29
Lynn, Jeffrey, 89

M

MacAfee, Kim, 28–29
MacArthur, Douglas, 134
MacMurray, Fred, 33
Macy, Bill, 104
Macy, William H., 104
Madonna, 83
The Magnificent Seven, 72
Mahoney, John, 62
Major League Baseball, 83
Malden, Karl, 56, 75
Malone, Dorothy, 146
Maltin, Leonard, 3, 38
Mamet, David, 142–143
Mandel, Babaloo, 82
Mangold, James, 2
Mankiewicz, Joseph L., 88, 90
Man's Favorite Sport?, 119
March, Fredric, 55, 57
March, Joseph Moncure, 121
Marlowe, Hugh, 54, 140–141
Married to the Mob, 91–93
Marshall, Penny, 82
Martin, Dean, 101, 118–119
Martin, Dewey, 56
Martin, Lock, 53
Marvin, Lee, 14
Mary Poppins, 77
The Mary Tyler Moore Show, 27
*M*A*S*H*, 76
Mason, James, 142–143
Masterpiece Theater, 106
Mathews, Charles, 8, 90
Mature, Victor, 79
Maude, 104

Maurer, David S., 129
Maverick, 71
Maxwell, Marilyn, 85–86
Mayer, Louis B., 134
Mayes, Wendell, 9
McCallum, David, 71
McCarthy, Eugene, 35
McCarthy, Joseph, 9
McCarthy, Kevin, 59
McDonald, Christopher, 114
McKay, Jim, 19, 21
McQueen, Steve, 70–72
Melvin and Howard, 92
Merrill, Gary, 140
Middleton, Robert, 41, 56
Miracle on 34th Street, 81, 94–96
Miranda, Carmen, 46
Mitchell, Ellen, 49–50
Mitchum, Robert, 43–44, 120, 138
Moby Dick, 140
Modine, Matthew, 91–92
Montgomery, Robert, 133–135
Moonstruck, ii, 27
Morgan, David Lee, 125
Morgan, Nathan Lee, 124–126
Morgan, Rebecca, 124–125
Morison, Patricia, 80
Moross, Jerome, 21
Morrow, Rob, 112–113
Mr. Smith Goes to Washington, 36
Munro, Rachel, 37–39
Munro, Rupert, 38
Murphy's Romance, 97–99
The Music Man, 100–102
Mutiny on the Bounty, 108

My Fair Lady, 102
My Favorite Year, 103–105
My Left Foot, 111

N

The Naked Gun, 151
Natwick, Mildred, 41–42
Neal, Patricia, 52–54
Nelson, Ricky, 119
Nemerov, Howard, 130
Nevins, Larry, 22–24
Newman, Paul, 4, 6, 56, 105, 127–129, 142–144
Nicholson, Jack, 18, 104, 128, 144
Nielsen, Leslie, 148–149, 151
Nightmare Alley, 81
Nixon, Richard, 36, 57
Nolan, Lloyd, 86
Norma Rae, 98
Nostromo, 108
North, Edmund, 52–53
Nozik, Michael, 112

O

O'Brien, Robert, 85
O'Connell, Arthur, 8
O'Hara, Maureen, 94–95
On the Waterfront, 58, 60
Ordinary People, 128
Osborne, Barrie M., 37
Osborne, Robert, 15
O'Shea, Milo, 144
O'Toole, Peter, 103–105

P

Pakula, Alan J., 109–110
Palumbo, Dennis, 103–104
Panama, Norman, 40–41
Parker, Cecil, 42
Pasternak, Joe, 46, 48
The Patriot, 77
Patten, Luana, 76, 78
Paxton, Bill, 10–11
Paxton, John, 43–44
Paymer, David, 113
Payne, John, 81, 95
Pearson, Jesse, 30
Peck, Gregory, 19, 21, 139, 141
Perkins, Anthony, 32, 130
Perlberg, William, 94
Pesci, Joe, 67–68
Petty, Lori, 83
Pfeiffer, Michelle, 91, 93
Phillips, Julia, 127
Phillips, Michael, 127
The Piano, 27
Pickup on South Street, 81
Pierson, Frank, 109–110
Pileggi, Nicholas, 67
Pillsbury, Sarah, 61
The Pink Panther, 59
Place, Mary Kay, 17
Places in the Heart, 98
Platoon, 76
Platt, Oliver, 92
Pollack, Sydney, 4–5, 109–110
Porter, Don, 36
Powell, Jane, 46, 48
Preminger, Otto, 7
Prentiss, Paula, 119
Presley, Elvis, 29
Preston, Robert, 100-102
Presumed Innocent, ii, 109–111
Previn, André, 14
Primary Colors, 35
The Prisoner of Zenda, 50
Psycho, i, 103, 117, 131
Pullman, Bill, 83

Q

Queeg, Philip, 31–33
Quine, Richard, 58, 60
Quinlan, Kathleen, 11
Quinn, Anthony, 147
Quiz Show, ii, 112–114

R

Radnitz, Robert B., 124
Raging Bull, 121
Rains, Claude, 52
Rampling, Charlotte, 142, 144
Rathbone, Basil, 41
Rau, Santha Rama, 106
Ravetch, Irving, 97–98
Rear Window, i, 58, 115–117
Red River, 81, 119
Redford, Robert, 34, 36, 112, 127–128, 131, 144
Reed, Barry, 142
Reed, Carol, 136–137
Reed, Donna, 135
Reitman, Ivan, 49
Remick, Lee, 7–8
Rennie, Michael, 52–53, 138

Revere, Paul, 77–78, 113
The Right Stuff, 11
Rio Bravo, i, 118–120
Rio Lobo, 120
Ritchie, Michael, 34–35
Ritt, Martin, 97–98, 124–125
Ritter, Thelma, 90, 96, 116
Rivera, Chita, 29
Roberts, Julia, 111
Roberts, Stanley, 31
Robson, Mark, 22–24
Roman Holiday, 21
Rooney, Mickey, 58–59
Rosenberg, Mark, 109–110
Ross, Gary, 49
Rotten Tomatoes, 1, 38, 99
Rubin, Steven Jay, 54
Ruehl, Mercedes, 92
Runyon, Damon, 85–86
Russell, John, 119
Ryan, Robert, 13–14, 43–44, 121–122
Ryan's Daughter, 107
Rydell, Bobby, 29

S

Sabich, Rusty, 109–111
Samuels, Joseph, 44
Sande, Walter, 78
Saving Private Ryan, 76, 134
Saxon, Edward, 91
Sayles, John, 17, 61
Scacchi, Greta, 110
Schary, Dore, 13–14, 45
Schenck, Nicholas, 14
Schott, Max, 97

Schwary, Ronald, 4
Scofield, Paul, 113
Scorsese, Martin, ii, 67, 80, 91, 113
Scott, Adrian, 43, 45
Scott, George C., 8
Scott, Martha, 56
The Searchers, ii
Seaton, George, 94–95
Selznick, David O., 117, 136–137
The Set-Up, 121–123
Shagan, Steve, 129
Shamberg, Michael, 16
Shaw, Robert, 64, 66, 128
Sheen, Charlie, 62
Sidney, George, 28–29
Siegel, Sol, 88
Silverado, 18
Simmons, Jean, 19–20
Simpson, Alan, 51
Sinatra, Frank, 3, 101
Sinise, Gary, 11
Sirk, Douglas, 145–146
Some Came Running, 3
Something Wild, 92
Sommer, Josef, 5
Sophie's Choice, 51
Sorvino, Paul, 68
Sothern, Ann, 88–89
Sounder, 124–126
Splendor in the Grass, 131
Stack, Robert, 46, 145–147, 149
Stalmaster, Hal, 76, 78
A Star is Born, 58
Steinberg, Norman, 103–104
Stevenson, Robert, 76–77

Stewart, James, 7–9, 36, 59, 115–117, 132, 138
Stewart, Michael, 28
The Sting, i, 127–129
The Sting II, 129
Stockwell, Dean, 92
Stovall, Harvey, 139, 141
Stowe, Madeleine, 37–39
Strathairn, David, 61–62
Streep, Meryl, 6, 51, 81
Strouse, Charles, 28
Strugatz, Barry, 91
Stryker, Ted, 148–149
Sturges, John, 13–14, 70–71
Sweeney, D.B., 61–62
Swigert, Jack, 10–11

T

Tabori, George, 73, 75
The Taking of Pelham 123, 129
Tall Story, 130–132
Taps, Jonie, 58
Tashlin, Frank, 85, 87
Taylor, Elizabeth, 46–47
Terkel, Studs, 62
Terms of Endearment, 27
Terrell, Stephen, 143
They Were a Team, 134
They Were Expendable, 133–135
They Were Professionals, 134
The Third Man, i, 136–138
Thorpe, Richard, 46–47
Tighe, Kevin, 63
Tilly, Jennifer, 17
Titanic, 99

To Kill a Mockingbird, 141
Tobias, George, 122
Toone, Geoffrey, 149
Tootsie, 105
Totter, Audrey, 121–123
Tracy, Spencer, 13–14, 52, 59, 135
Traver, Robert, 7
Travis, Nancy, 92
Trowbridge, Charles, 135
True Grit, 80
Tunney, John, 35
Turner, Kathleen, 38
Turner, Lana, 9
Turow, Scott, 109
Turturro, John, 112–113
Twelve O'Clock High, 139–141
Twenty-One, 112–113
Tyson, Cicely, 124–125

U

Udo, Tommy, 79, 81
The Untouchables, 143
USA Today, 62, 140
Utt, Kenneth, 91

V

Valley Forge General Hospital, 23
Valli, Alida, 137
Van Dyke, Dick, 28–30
Vankin, Jonathan, 68
The Verdict, 4–5, 105, 142–144
Vertigo, ii
Vietnam War, 85
Viva Las Vegas, 30

W

Walston, Ray, 129
War of 1812, 78
Ward, David S., 127–128
Warden, Jack, 143
Warner, Jack, 100, 102
Washington, Denzel, 64–66
Wayne, John, 1, 14, 80–81, 118, 120, 133
Wead, Frank, 133
Weaver, Sigourney, 49–50
Webb, James R., 19
Welch, Joseph N., 9
Welch, Robert, 85
Welles, Orson, 136–138
Whalen, John, 68
White Christmas, 41
White, William Lindsay, 133
Who the Devil Made It, 74
Widmark, Richard, 79, 81
Wiest, Dianne, 111
Wilder, Robert, 19, 145
Williams, JoBeth, 17
Williams, John, 110
Williams, Robin, 32, 41, 104
Willis, Gordon, 110
Willson, Meredith, 100–101
Wilson, Kim, 82
Winfield, Paul, 110, 124–126
Winger, Debra, 27, 83
Winkler, Irwin, 67
Wise, Robert, 52–53, 121
Wiseguy, 67–68
Wood, Natalie, 94–96
Woolrich, Cornell, 115–116
World War II, 13–14, 23–24, 32, 42, 71, 74, 82, 133–134, 136, 139–140, 149
Wouk, Herman, 31–32
Wrigley, Phil, 83
Written on the Wind, i, 145–147
The Wrong Man, 73–74
Wyler, William, 19, 55–56
Wynn, May, 32

Y

York, Jeff, 78
Young, Gig, 56
Young, Robert, 43–45

Z

Zanuck, Darryl F., 53, 90, 94, 139
Zanuck, Richard, 142, 144
Zero Hour!, 148–151
Ziskin, Laura, 97
Zucker, David, 148, 150
Zucker, Jerry, 148, 150
Zuckerman, George, 145
Zugsmith, Albert, 145
Zwick, Edward, 64–65

PHOTO CREDITS

PAGE	
1	Columbia Pictures/Photofest ©Columbia Pictures
4	Columbia Pictures/Photofest ©Columbia Pictures
7	Photofest
10	Universal Pictures/Photofest ©Universal Pictures
13	MGM/Photofest ©MGM
16	Columbia Pictures/Photofest ©Columbia Pictures
19	United Artists/Photofest ©United Artists
22	Universal Pictures/Photofest ©Universal Pictures
25	20th Century Fox/Photofest ©20th Century Fox
28	Columbia Pictures/Photofest ©Columbia Pictures
31	Columbia Pictures/Photofest ©Columbia Pictures
34	Warner Bros. Pictures/Photofest ©Warner Bros. Pictures
37	Orion Pictures Corporation/Photofest ©Orion Pictures Corporation
40	Paramount Pictures/Photofest ©Paramount Pictures
43	RKO Radio Pictures/Photofest ©RKO Radio Pictures
46	MGM/Photofest ©MGM
49	Warner Bros. Pictures/Photofest ©Warner Bros. Pictures
52	20th Century Fox/Photofest ©20th Century Fox

PAGE	
55	Paramount Pictures/Photofest ©Paramount Pictures
58	Columbia Pictures/Photofest ©Columbia Pictures
61	Orion Classics/Photofest ©Orion Classics
64	TriStar Pictures/Photofest ©TriStar Pictures Photographer: Merrick Morton
67	Warner Bros. Pictures/Photofest ©Warner Bros. Pictures Photographer: Barry Wetcher
70	United Artists/Photofest ©United Artists
73	Warner Bros. Pictures/Photofest ©Warner Bros. Pictures
76	Walt Disney Pictures/Photofest ©Walt Disney Pictures
79	20th Century Fox/Photofest ©20th Century Fox
82	Columbia Pictures/Photofest ©Columbia Pictures
85	Paramount Pictures/Photofest ©Paramount Pictures
88	20th Century Fox/Photofest ©20th Century Fox
91	Orion/Photofest ©Orion
94	20th Century Fox/Photofest ©20th Century Fox
97	Columbia Pictures/Photofest ©Columbia Pictures
100	Warner Bros. Pictures/Photofest ©Warner Bros. Pictures

PAGE

103	MGM/UA/Photofest ©MGM/UA
106	Columbia Pictures/Photofest ©Columbia Pictures
109	Warner Bros. Pictures/Photofest ©Warner Bros. Pictures
112	Buena Vista Pictures/Photofest ©Buena Vista Pictures
115	Paramount Pictures/Photofest ©Paramount Pictures
118	Warner Bros. Pictures/Photofest ©Warner Bros. Pictures
121	RKO/Photofest ©RKO
124	20th Century Fox/Photofest ©20th Century Fox
127	Universal Pictures/Photofest ©Universal Pictures
130	Warner Bros. Pictures/Photofest ©Warner Bros. Pictures
133	MGM/Photofest ©MGM
136	Selznick Releasing Organization /Photofest ©Selznick Releasing Organization
139	20th Century Fox/Photofest ©20th Century Fox
142	20th Century Fox/Photofest ©20th Century Fox
145	Universal Pictures/Photofest ©Universal Pictures
148	Paramount Pictures/Photofest ©Paramount Pictures
150	Paramount Pictures/Photofest ©Paramount Pictures

ACKNOWLEDGEMENTS

Thanks to John Hughes; Doug Barker; Jeff Burlingame; Lisa Patterson; Kat Bryant; Janet Simmelink; Rob Burns; Karen & Mike Barkstrom; Dan Jackson; Carl Molesworth; Glen Potter; Gail Greenwood Ayres; Pam Blair; David Haerle; John Larson and the Polson Museum; Ed Klein; Alex Schloer; Sandy Deneau Dunham; Gorham Printing; John Rodin; Jaimie Brand, Mickey Thurman, and Hoquiam's 7th Street Theatre Association; the staff at the Timberland Regional Library branches in Aberdeen, Hoquiam, and Montesano; the late Ray Ryan; the late Robert Arthur; my late parents, Earl and Erma Anderson; my late brother, Jack; and my late sister, Judy Stavheim.

Plus some people I've never met — the hosts and researchers at Turner Classic Movies and the late Roger Ebert (the gold standard for film criticism). ∎

ABOUT THE AUTHOR

Rick Anderson is an award-winning journalist who has spent more than fifty years in the field, mostly as an editor and film critic at *The Daily World* newspaper in Aberdeen, Washington. His favorite genres include mysteries, thrillers, films noir, historical dramas, sports films, and comedies. His all-time Academy Award choices would include Alec Guinness for *The Bridge on the River Kwai,* Holly Hunter for *Broadcast News,* Angela Lansbury for the 1962 version of *The Manchurian Candidate*, and Fred MacMurray for *The Caine Mutiny.* ∎

www.ingramcontent.com/pod-product-compliance
Lightning Source LLC
Chambersburg PA
CBHW072004290426
44109CB00018B/2124